Freedom

Concepts in the Social Sciences

Series Editor: Frank Parkin
Magdalen College, Oxford

Published Titles

Democracy	*Anthony Arblaster*
Citizenship	*J. M. Barbalet*
Freedom	*Zygmunt Bauman*
Bureaucracy	*David Beetham*
Socialism	*Bernard Crick*
Liberalism	*John Gray*
Ideology	*David McLellan*
Conservatism	*Robert Nisbet*
Race and Ethnicity	*John Rex*
Property	*Alan Ryan*
Status	*Bryan S. Turner*

Forthcoming Titles

Nationalism	*Hamza Alavi*
Fascism	*Robert Benewick*
Exchange	*John Davis*
Rights	*Michael Freeden*
The State	*John Hall and John Ikenberry*
Leninism	*Neil Harding*
Kinship	*Chris Harris*
Utopianism	*Krishan Kumar*
Gender	*Mary McIntosh*
Capitalism	*Göran Therborn*
Charisma	*Roy Wallis*

Concepts in the Social Sciences

Freedom

Zygmunt Bauman

Open University Press

Milton Keynes

Open University Press
Open University Educational Enterprises Limited
12 Cofferidge Close
Stony Stratford
Milton Keynes MK11 1BY, England

First Published 1988

British Library Cataloguing in Publication Data

Bauman, Zygmunt
 Freedom. – (Concepts in the social sciences).
 1. Freedom. Theories
 I. Title.   II. Series
 323.44′01

ISBN 0-335-15592-8
ISBN 0-335-15591-X Pbk

Typeset by Scarborough Typesetting Services
Printed in Great Britain by J. W. Arrowsmith Ltd., Bristol

Contents

Introduction

'You can say what you wish. This is a free country'. We use and hear this expression too often to pause and think of its meaning; we take it as obvious, self-explanatory, presenting no problem to our, or to our partner's, understanding. In a sense, freedom is like the air we breathe. We don't ask what this air is, we do not spend time discussing it, arguing about it, thinking of it. That is, unless we are in a crowded, stuffy room and find breathing difficult.

This book sets out to show that what we consider to be evident and clear (if we consider it at all) is far from being so; that its apparent familiarity comes merely from its frequent use (and abuse, as we will see); that it has a long and chequered, rarely recalled, history; that it is much more ambiguous a thing than we are ready to admit; that, in short, there is more to freedom than meets the eye.

Let us return for a moment to the expression with which we started. What does it tell us if we listen carefully?

It tells us, first, that in a condition of freedom you and I may do what under a different condition would be either impossible or risky. We *can* do what we wish, without fear of being punished, thrown in jail, tortured, persecuted. Let us note, however, that the expression is silent about how effective our action will be. 'Free country' does not guarantee that what we do will reach its purpose, or what we say will be accepted. Indeed, what the expression tacitly admits is that the truth or wisdom of our statements is not a condition of making them; and that an action does not have to be reasonable to be allowed.

And so the expression tells us also that being in a *free* country means doing things on one's own responsibility. One is free to pursue (and, with luck, to achieve) one's aims, but one is also free to err. The first comes with the second, in a package deal. Being free, you can be sure that no one will prohibit the action you wish to undertake. But you are not offered any certainty that what you wish to do, and do, will bring you the benefit you expect, or benefit at all for that matter.

Our expression suggests that the only thing which matters in making and keeping you free is that the 'free society', that is a society of free individuals, does not forbid you to act on your wishes and refrains from punishing you for such acts. Here, however, the message becomes misleading. Lack of prohibition or punitive sanctions is indeed a necessary condition for acting according to one's wishes, but not a sufficient one. You may be free to leave the country at will, but have no money for the ticket. You may be free to seek skills in the field of your choice, but find that there is no place for you where you want to study. You may wish to work in a job which interests you, but find no such job available. You may say what you wish, only to find out that there is no way to make yourself audible. Thus freedom has more to it than lack of restrictions. To do things, one needs *resources*. Our expression does not promise you such resources, but pretends — wrongly — that this does not matter.

There is one more message one can read from our expression with some extra effort. This is a statement the expression neither asserts nor denies, overtly or tacitly, but simply takes for granted, as an assumption one can make without discussion. What our expression takes for granted is that given the chance, one will indeed 'say what one wishes' and 'do what one wishes'. That, in other words, a human individual is — as if 'by nature' — the true source and master of his/her doings and thoughts; that left to one's own discretion one would shape and mould one's thoughts and acts at will, according to one's own intention.

This image of the individual guided by his/her motives, of the individual action as an *intended* or *intentional* action, an action 'with an author', could have been taken for granted because it has been firmly settled in the common sense of the kind of society we live in. This is indeed the way all of us think about people and their behaviour. We ask ourselves, 'What did he mean?'; 'What was he after?'; 'What has he done it for?' — thus assuming that actions are effects of the actor's intentions and purposes, and that to 'make sense' of an action one needs to go no further than such intentions and purposes. Since we believe that one's motives are the causes of one's action, we assume also that the whole and undivided responsibility for the action lies with its perpetrator (providing he or she were not 'forced' to do what they did, i.e. they were free).

Supported by common sense (i.e. by everybody else's opinions) our beliefs seem to us so well founded — indeed, self-evident — that on the whole we refrain from asking searching questions about their validity. We do not ask where such beliefs have come from in the first place and what sort of experience maintains their credibility. So we may overlook the connection between our beliefs and quite peculiar features of our own — Western, modern, capitalist — society. We may, and we do, remain unaware that the experience which supplies ever new proofs for our beliefs comes from the legal framework which this particular society set for human life. It is this particular law which names the individual human being as the subject of rights, obligations and responsibilities; which holds the individual, and the individual alone, responsible for his or her actions; which defines the action as a kind of behaviour which has the intention of the actor as its ultimate cause and explanation. It is this particular law which explains what has happened by the purpose the actor set for himself. What creates the experience which keeps corroborating our beliefs is of course not the legal theory (most of us have never heard of it) but the practice which follows it — individuals signing contracts in their own name, taking obligations upon themselves, bearing responsibility for their deeds. We see this happening all around and all the time; and so we have no chance to notice the peculiarity of it. We see it rather as something which manifests 'the nature of things', the universal, immutable 'essence' of human beings.

Through most of its history, sociology was no more universal than our commonsensical beliefs or the man-made social realities which support them. Sociology emerged originally out of the experience of the Western, modern capitalist society and the problems this experience put on the agenda. The experience came, so to speak, pre-packed, pre-interpreted; that is to say, complete with common-sensical beliefs which had already made the experience intelligible in their own peculiar but firmly entrenched way. This is why, when trying to think through the working of their society in an orderly, systematic fashion, sociologists tended to follow common sense in taking it as an axiom that individuals are 'normally' the sources of their own actions; that actions are shaped by the purposes and intentions of the actors; that the actor's motives supply the ultimate explanations of the course the action has taken. The free will and uniqueness of each and any individual were seen as 'brute facts' of a sort, as a product of nature rather than of specific social arrangements.

It is partly due to such an assumption that the attention of sociologists turned to 'unfreedom' rather than freedom; if the latter was a fact of nature, the former must have been an artificial creation, a product of certain social arrangements, hence sociologically most interesting. In the magnificent legacy the founders of sociology left us, 'freedom' appears relatively seldom. In the main body of social theory, serious considerations of the 'social conditioning' of freedom are few, far between and marginal. On the other hand, there is a lot of interest in, and profound observations about, 'social constraints', pressures, influences, power, coercion and whatever other man-made factors were blamed for preventing freedom, that natural endowment of every human being, from manifesting itself.

Leaving freedom out of focus and concentrating instead on its limitations, should not surprise us. The assumption of free will made social order a puzzle. Looking around themselves, sociologists could not help but note, much like ordinary people do, that somehow human conduct is regular, follows some patterns, is by and large predictable; there is some regularity in the society as a whole — some events are much more likely to happen than some others. Whence such a regularity, if every individual within the society is unique, and each pursues his own purposes, exercising free will? The fact that human action, assumed to be voluntary, was evidently not random, appeared a mystery. Another, more practical consideration added to the energy with which sociologists set about the exploration of the 'frontiers of freedom'. Together with other thinkers of the Enlightenment era, sociologists wished not only to explore the world but to make it a better place for humans to live. In this perspective, free will of the individual appeared a mixed blessing. With everybody pursuing their own interests only, common interests could find themselves poorly served. With individuals free as they inescapably are, the proper maintenance of order in society as a whole ought to be made an object of special effort, and hence also of diligent study. Again, what one needs to study is the way in which at least some (socially harmful) individual intentions can be tempered, defused or downright suppressed. Thus intense interest in limitations of freedom had both cognitive and normative justifications.

It was for these reasons that sociology developed as a 'science of unfreedom' first and foremost. The main concern of well-nigh every project of sociology as a separate programme of scientific investigation was to find out why human individuals, being free, act nevertheless in a nearly regular, more or less constant, way. Or, to consider the same question from a normative point of view, what conditions must be met to prompt the actions of free individuals in a specific direction?

And so the concepts like class, power, domination, authority, socialization, ideology, culture and education organized the sociological map of the human world. What all these and similar concepts had in common was the idea of an external pressure which sets the limits to individual will or interferes with the actual (as distinct from the intended) action. The shared quality of the phenomena which such concepts postulated was that they changed the direction of individual actions compared to the course those actions would have taken if external pressures had been absent. Cumulatively, the concepts in question were meant to explain the relative non-randomness, the regularity of conduct in individuals allegedly acting upon their own, private motives and interests. Let us remember that this latter assertion was not an object of study or explanation; it entered sociological discourse as a self-evident, axiomatic assumption.

One can divide the concepts related to the external, extra-individual pressures into two broad categories. The first group of concepts construes a series of 'external constraints' — much like the almost physical, tangible resistance a slab of marble puts to the fantasy of the sculptor. External constraints are those elements of outer reality which classify individual intentions into feasible and unrealistic, and the situations the individual wishes to attain through his actions into highly probable or very unlikely. The individual still pursues freely chosen aims, and yet his well-intended efforts collapse as they collide with the solid rock or impenetrable wall of power, class or coercive apparatus. The second group of concepts relates to those regulatory forces which tend to be 'internalized' by the individuals. Through training, drilling, instructing or just through an example set by the people around, the very motives, expectations, hopes and ambitions of the individual are shaped in a peculiar fashion, so that their direction is not fully random from the start. Such a 'de-randomization' is postulated by concepts like 'culture', 'tradition' or 'ideology'. All such concepts envisage a hierarchy in the social production of beliefs and motives. All wills are free, but some wills are freer than others: some people, who knowingly or unknowingly perform the function of educators, instil (or modify) the cognitive predispositions, moral values and aesthetic preferences of others and thus introduce certain shared elements into their intentions and ensuing actions.

Thus human actions are regularized by supra-individual forces which come overtly from outside (as constraints), or ostensibly from inside (as life-project or conscience). Such forces fully account for the observed non-randomness of human conduct, and so we have no need to revise our original assumptions, that is our vision of human beings as individuals armed with free will, determining their actions through their own motives, aims and interests.

Sociology, let us recall, emerged as a reflection on a particular kind of society: the society which established itself in the West during the modern era, in conjunction with the development of capitalism. A guess that the constitution of human beings as free individuals has something to do with the peculiar features of this kind of society (rather than being a universal attribute of the human species) cannot be rejected out of hand. If the guess is true, then the free individual will appear a historical creation, much like the society to which he belongs. And the connections between such a free individual and the society of which he is a member will be much stronger and more essential than many a sociologist assumed. The relevance of society will not be confined to erecting barriers to individual pursuits and to the 'cultural regulation' or 'ideological direction' of individual motives. It will pertain to the very existence of human beings as free individuals. Not only the way in which the free individual operates but the very identity of men and women as free individuals will be recognized as constituted by the society.

The historically and spatially restricted incidence of free individuality was difficult to discover and understand from inside a discourse confined to a similarly restricted experience. How difficult it was, you and I are in a good position to judge. A 'non-individual' human being, a human who is not a free-chooser, preoccupied with establishing his own identity, with his own welfare and satisfaction, we cannot truly imagine. He finds no resonance in our own life experience. He is a monster, an incongruity.

Yet historical and anthropological studies keep supplying evidence that this 'natural' free individual of ours is a rather rare species and a local phenomenon. A very special concatenation of circumstances was necessary to bring him into being; and it is only with these circumstances persisting that he can survive. The free individual, far from being a universal condition of humankind, is a historical and social creation.

This last sentence can be taken as the central topic of this book. The intention behind the book is, so to speak, to render 'the familiar' strange; to see freedom of the individual (something we normally take for granted, as a quality which can be tampered with or thwarted, but which is 'always there') as a puzzle, as a phenomenon which must be accounted for, explained in order to be understood. The message of the book is that individual freedom cannot and should not be taken for granted, as it appears (and perhaps disappears) together with a particular kind of a society.

We will see that freedom exists only as a social relation; that instead of being a property, a possession of the individual himself, it is a quality pertaining to a certain difference between individuals; that it makes sense only as an opposition to some other condition, past or present. We will see that the existence of free individuals signals a differentiation of statuses within a given society and that, moreover, it plays a crucial role in stabilizing and reproducing such a differentiation.

We will see that freedom widespread enough to appear as a universal human condition is a relative novelty in the history of human species, a novelty closely connected with the advent of modernity and capitalism. We will also see that freedom could make this claim to universality only once it had acquired the peculiar meaning tied inextricably to life conditions in the capitalist society, and that its peculiarly modern connotation of 'ability to master one's own fate' was intimately related at its birth to those preoccupations with the artificiality of social order which were the most distinctive characteristics of modern times.

We will see that freedom in our society is simultaneously a condition indispensable for social integration and systemic reproduction, and a condition continuously recreated by the way society is integrated and the system 'works'. This centrality of individual freedom as a link holding together the individual life-world, society and the social system has been attained with the recent shift of freedom away from the area of production and power and into the area of consumption. In our society, individual freedom is constituted as, first and foremost, freedom of the consumer; it hangs upon the presence of an effective market, and in its turn assures the conditions of such a presence.

We will explore in the end the consequences of this form of freedom for other dimensions of social reality, and above all for the character of contemporary politics and the role of the state. We will explore the possibility that with individual freedom firmly established in its consumer form, the state tends to distance itself from its traditional concerns with the 'recommodification' of capital and labour and with legitimizing the structure of dominance — the first becoming less relevant to the reproduction of the system, and the second resolved in a non-political form through the consumer market. The next possibility explored will be the causal connection between the fading of traditional state functions and the growing independence of the state from social, democratic control. We will try to comprehend the emerging social arrangement as a system in its own right, instead of viewing it as a diseased, disorganized or otherwise terminally ill form of the earlier modern-capitalist society. We will also look briefly at the inner logic of the communist form of modern society, and the consequences of the absence of consumer freedom for the plight of the individual.

Panopticon, or Freedom as Social Relation

Freedom was born as a privilege and has remained so ever since. Freedom divides and separates. It sets the best apart from the rest. It draws its attraction from difference: its presence or absence reflects, marks and grounds the contrast between high and low, good and bad, coveted and repugnant.

Originally and ever since, freedom has stood for the coexistence of two sharply distinct social conditions; to acquire freedom, to be free, meant to be lifted from one, inferior social condition to another, superior condition. The two conditions differed in many respects, but one aspect of their opposition — that captured by the quality of freedom — towered high above the rest: the difference between action dependent on the will of others and action dependent on one's own will.

For *one* to be free there must be at least *two*. Freedom signifies a social relation, an asymmetry of social conditions; essentially it implies social difference — it presumes and implies the presence of social division. Some can be free only in so far as there is a form of dependence they can aspire to escape. If being free means to be allowed to go anywhere (*OED* dates this use from 1483), it also means that there are people who are tied to their abode and denied the right to move freely. If being free means a release from ties and obligations (*OED*, 1596) or work and duty (*OED*, 1697), this makes sense only thanks to the others who are tied, who carry obligations, who work and have duties. If being free means acting without restriction (*OED*, 1578), it implies that the actions of some others are constrained. In Old and Middle English, freedom always meant an exemption — from tax, toll, duty, jurisdiction of a lord. Exemption, in its turn, meant privilege: to be free meant to be admitted to exclusive rights — of a corporation, of a city, of an estate. Those so exempt and privileged joined the ranks of the noble and the honourable. Up to the end of the sixteenth century 'freedom' was synonymous with gentle birth or breeding, nobility, generosity, magnanimity — of every trait the mighty and the powerful claimed as the sign and the reason of their exclusivity and superiority. Later it lost its link with noble birth. But it retained its meaning of privilege. The discourse of freedom focused now on the question of *who* has the right to be free in an essentially unfree human condition.

Modern society differs from its predecessors by its gardener-like, rather than gamekeeper-like, attitude to itself. It views the maintenance of social order (i.e., the containment of human conduct within certain parameters, and the predictability of human behaviour within these parameters) as an 'issue': something to be kept on the agenda, considered, discussed, taken care of, dealt with, resolved. Modern society does not believe it can be secure without consciously and deliberately taking measures to safeguard its security. These measures mean, first and foremost, the guiding and monitoring of human conduct: they mean social control. Social control, in its turn, may be exercised in two ways. One can put people in a situation which prevents them from doing things one doesn't wish them to do; or put them in a situation which encourages them to do things one wishes them to do. One does not wish some things to be done as they are deemed to be detrimental to social order. One wishes other things to be done as they are deemed to perpetuate and reinvigorate the social order. Whether it is the undesirable conduct one wants to ward off or the desirable action one wants to prompt — the administration of the appropriate setting is the crucial task. But this task splits into two: prevention and encouragement. Prevention is the purpose of administration, if there is reason to believe that given the choice people would behave in a way contrary to the conduct the perpetuation of social order demands. Encouragement is the purpose, if some other people are trusted to embark, given the chance, on action seen as reinforcing the proper order of things. This is what the opposition between heteronomy and autonomy, control and self-control, regimentation and freedom, is about.

Michel Foucault's ingenious interpretation revealed the significance of Jeremy Bentham's *Panopticon* (the full title: *Panopticon; or, the Inspection House, containing the Idea of a new Principle of Construction applicable to any Sort of Establishment, in which persons of any description are to be kept under Inspection and in particular to Penitentiary-House, Prisons, Houses of Industry, Work-Houses, Poor-Houses, Manufactories, Mad-Houses, Lazarettos, Hospitals, and Schools: with a Plan of Management adapted to the Principle*[1]) as an insight into the disciplinary nature of modern power, management of the bodies as its paramount purpose and surveillance as its fundamental technique. What this interpretation left out of sight, however, was that in addition to all that — in itself no mean achievement — the *Panopticon* was an insight into the *opposition* between freedom and unfreedom, the autonomous and the regimented action; that this opposition was revealed to be not simply a logical distinction between two idealized types but a social *relationship* between mutually determining positions inside one social structure; and that both sides of the opposition, in their intimate and intricate relationship, were shown to be a product of scientific management of sorts, of a purposeful *administration* of social conditions, conceived and monitored by experts armed with specialist knowledge and the power to act on it.

The inmates of the panopticon (this universal 'control machine') are defined solely by the intention their confinement should serve — the intention, of course, of those who put them there. The inmates are *objects*, of 'safe custody, confinement, solitude, forced labour, and instruction'; the intention behind their condition is to transform them into something they are not and something they themselves have no intention of becoming. It is because of this absence of will that they have been made inmates in the first place. The conditions under which they are put while confinement must be carefully calculated so as to serve best the purposes of those who confined them — purposes like 'punishing the incorrigible, guarding the insane, reforming the vicious, confining the suspected, employing the idle, maintaining the helpless, curing the sick, instructing the willing in any branch of industry or training the rising race in the path of education';[2] depending on its purpose, the confinement varies its social identity. It can become 'perpetual prisons in the room of death, or prisons for confinement before trial, or penitentiary-houses, or houses of correction, or work-houses, or manufactories, or mad-houses, or hospitals, or schools'. The conditions of the confined, however, do not vary with the social identity of the confinement.

What follows is that social conditions appropriate to various categories of inmates are not measured by the intrinsic qualities of the latter (e.g. whether they are old or young, healthy or sick, guilty of a crime or not, morally contemptible or innocent, corrupt beyond repair or in need of correction, deserving punishment or care), but by the coordination (or rather its absence) between the likely actions of the inmates when left to their own devices and the conduct the purposes of their confinement would require. It does not matter whether the suspected discrepancy between the two ought to be ascribed to the inmates' ill will or to their bodily or spiritual infirmity or to their psychological immaturity or imperfection. The only thing which does matter is that the desired conduct can be elicited only by the will of others — the will of the inmates being either absent or deliberately 'switched off' or suppressed.

What unites the inmates of the panopticon (whatever its contingent — functional — assignment) is the supervisor's intention to substitute the will of the inspectors for the missing or unreliable will of the inmates. It is the will of the inspectors (prison guards, foremen, doctors, teachers) which ought to define, guide and monitor the conduct of the inmates. Let us note that it does not matter what the inmates *feel* about things they are commanded to do; it does not matter either whether they consider the commands as *legitimate* or whether they 'internalize' and make into their own the intentions of their inspectors. Panopticon is not concerned with what the inmates think — only with what they do. Ideological domination, cultural hegemony, indoctrination, or whatever else the effort to attain spiritual subordination is called, would seem within the context of the panopticon an irrelevant and unjustifiable oddity. No one would ask whether the inmates will in the end do whatever they will do willingly — providing they do it.

Paring the matter of moral reform to the bare bones of heteronomy of behaviour was likely to invite the charge of cynicism. It flew too openly in the face of liberal pretensions, jarred too stridently with the rhetoric of the morally sovereign individual. Bentham had anticipated the charge and resolved to confront it point blank. To pre-empt the rage of the liberal critics he articulated their doubts for them: 'Whether the liberal spirit and energy of a free citizen would not be exchanged for the mechanical discipline of a soldier, or the austerity of a monk? — and whether the result of this high-wrought contrivance might not be constructing a set of *machines* under the similitude of *men*?'. And he proceeded to provide what he saw as the clinching proof that the doubts were unfounded and the fears misdirected:

To give a satisfactory answer to all these queries, which are mighty fine, but do not any of them come home to the point, it would be necessary to recur at once to the end of education. Would *happiness* be most likely to be increased or diminished by this discipline? — Call them soldiers, call them monks, call them machines: so they were but happy ones, I should not care. Wars and storms are best to read of, but peace and calms are better to enjoy.[3]

'The liberal spirit of a free citizen' would not, in all probability, be cultivated by the panopticon. But peace and calm it will guarantee, and with it the happiness of the inmates. What peace and calm panopticon-style connote, one has no difficulty in concluding from the totality of Bentham's plea, remarkable in its unity and consistency of argument. The condition of 'peace and calm' has two faces. Objectively it is characterized by the regularity, steadiness and predictability of the external context of inmates' action. Nothing is left to chance, and no realistic alternatives burden the inmates with the necessity of choice. There is nothing to hope for, but nothing to fear either. Subjectively the condition of 'peace and calm' means the inmates are reassured that their conduct is not at odds with their inspectors' demands, and hence unlikely to incur the wrath, complete with the punishment the inspectors would lavish on the insubordinate. Since the superiors require no more than conformity of behaviour, the art of making the flow of rewards steady is easy to learn and embroils the learner in no conflict, as it involves no contradiction or moral ambiguity. Between themselves the two faces of 'peace and calm' supply both the necessary and the sufficient ingredients of happiness. 'Sovereignty of the individual', freedom of choice, are not among them.

Bentham's inmate is not, however, a puppet with limbs moved by external strings alone. Inmates are supposed to be thinking and calculating beings; they are making choices, and their conduct is always a product of one. They also strive for happiness, like all the rest of us. And they can be trusted with one thing: by and large, they would tend to make a decision bringing them more, rather than less, happiness. Yet choice-making is a means of pursuing happiness, not the happiness itself. Choice-makers would for this reason prefer that 'peace and calm' which, once attained, leaves no room and need for choice.

The designer of the panopticon can easily guarantee the regularity of that preference simply by rendering the advantages of 'peace and calm' all the more protruding — through allowing only the most unappetizing alternative. He assures the future supervisor of the panopticon (worried as the latter might be about the feasibility of extracting useful and profitable labour from his wards) that no extra efforts would be required to supplement the pressures already contained in the tightly structured situation of the inmates. The future supervisor, in Bentham's words,

> will hardly think it necessary to ask me how he is to manage to persuade his borders to set to work. — Having them under this regimen, what better security he can wish for of their working, and that to their utmost, I can hardly imagine. At any rate, he has much better security that he can have for the industry and diligence of any ordinary journeyman at large, who is paid by the day, and not by the piece. If a man won't work nothing has he to do, from morning to night, but to eat his bad bread and drink his water, without a soul to speak to . . . This encouragement is necessary to his doing his utmost: but more than this is not necessary.[4]

Measured against bad bread, water and the loneliness of a single cell, any change — including that of hard labour and the utmost physical exertion — would feel like a reward. The choice is indeed simple, and even people devoid of the capacity for proper, useful behaviour can be trusted to display the right preference. The trust is founded in the very simplicity of the choice, not in the putative virtues of choosers. It is the task of the 'regimen', described under the name of panopticon, to guard this simplicity of choice. The task is fulfilled if, and only if, the regulations are aimed at prohibiting and eliminating all conduct they do not proclaim to be obligatory — and if they are backed by resources appropriate to make this intention realistic.

The gist of the *Panopticon* is to offer such resources which are foolproof and cheap; which render the task easy to achieve by reducing it to routine operations. Such resources, Bentham suggests, are generated by a certain organization of the space in which both the inmates and their supervisors are contained; in particular, by a specific design of the multi-purpose building. But behind this architectural device lies a principle much broader than its specific application limited by the technological horizons of its time.

In Bentham's own words, the essence of the panopticon consists in the '*centrality* of the inspector's situation, combined with the well-known and most effectual contrivances for *seeing without being seen*'. That is to say, the essence is the asymmetry of knowledge: the inspector knows everything about the inmates, while the inmates know nothing about the inspector. The whereabouts and the actions of the inspector are shrouded in mystery, invisible and hence unpredictable, while everything the inmate does is under constant scrutiny, permanently open to evaluation and corrective counteraction. Or so it must seem to the inmates, anyway. Actual continuous observation would be a good thing, but a very costly one — if at all attainable. Thus 'the next thing to be wished for', Bentham suggests, is that the inmate 'at every instant, seeing reason to believe as much, and not being able to satisfy himself to the contrary, he should *conceive* himself "to be under inspection"'.[5] Vulnerability of the inmate's privacy to the foreign gaze should be at any time a plausible supposition. Truly important is the '*apparent* omnipresence' (original emphasis) of the inspector. Once convinced that the eye of the superiors is always upon them, the inmates would never behave as if left to their own devices; they would have no occasion to exercise their own will, and thus their will would gradually flag and wither through lack of use. The permanence and the ubiquity of control will not merely deprive the inmates of their freedom: if effective, it will render the inmates *incapable* of being free, of choosing and guiding their own action, of structuring and administering their own life. They will now need the inspector to organize their lives for them; their particular kind of happiness, their 'peace and calm', will now require unfreedom, heteronomy, to be attained and to last. And all this miraculous reform will be accomplished without moral sermons, preaching ideals or engaging the soul and mind of the inmates in any other way. What is needed is merely an outward, behavioural control; and that depends solely on the proper organization of the network of external dependencies, with the asymmetry of access to information as its paramount principle.

'Seeing without being seen' makes the inspectors free *in relation to* the inmates they supervise. The freedom of the inspectors consists in this case in the independence of their action from what the inmates do or will, and in their ability to treat the inmates as the objects of their own will — their ability to influence and modify the inmates' action, to substitute their own will for the will of the inmates as the trigger and the determinant of the latter's conduct. The combination of the independence *from* and mastery *over* constitutes freedom of the inspectors *in relation to* the inmates. Freedom is one side of the relationship which has heteronomy and the absence of will as its other side. Inspectors are free in relation to the inmates in so far as freedom of action remains eliminated from the inmates' condition.

Being relational, the freedom of the inspectors points in one direction only. There are directions in which the almighty and omnipresent inspectors are unfree very much like the inmates are in relation to themselves. After all, the inspectors were put in the panopticon to perform a specific task not of their own choice: to watch and to command. The task is not necessarily intrinsically gratifying, being at best a satisfactory way to make a decent living — and thus the inspectors cannot be relied upon to refrain from doing rather less than the task demands — whenever they feel that they can get away with it. Hence one of the most puzzling of political questions, 'Quis custodiet ipsos custodes?', must be asked of the staff of the panopticon as much as any kind of people put in control of other people's behaviour. Yet the design of the panopticon takes account of the problem — and, so Bentham assures us, solves it in a most effective manner. In it, 'the *under*keepers or inspectors, the servants and subordinates of every kind, will be under the same irresistible control with respect to the *head*keeper or inspector, as the prisoners or other persons to be governed are with respect to them'.[6] Irresistible control of the inspectors is assured through the application of the same principle as in securing irresistible control of the inmates: through asymmetry of knowledge. The interior of the central lodge occupied by the inspector is opaque and invisible to the inmates; but it is wide open to the gaze of the headkeeper. The inspectors would not know when their supervisor chooses to watch them at work; he is free to do so whenever he wants without being seen himself. To the inspectors he is 'apparently omnipresent', just as the inspectors are to the inmates. This freedom of the head-keeper in relation to the inspectors imposes limits upon the relational freedom of the latter towards the inmates: one thing they are barred from including in their range of options is the choice not to exercise control over their wards; inspectors are not free to permit the freedom of the inmates. *Their* freedom, at least, is not complete. It cannot be allowed to be complete as the logic of the situation in which the inspectors are cast (as employees, as being entitled to an invariant income for their labour time, as treating their tasks as a job to be done for the ensuing remuneration, rather than for its inner attraction) does not guarantee that their conduct will normally concord with the purpose of the establishment they operate. Undesirable, harmful behaviour is a possibility one cannot preclude. Such behaviour must therefore be prevented artificially, through purposefully designed precautions. Hence the need of a setting which will determine the heteronomy of inspectors in one crucial aspect of their action.

The picture changes completely once we move one step further up, to that 'quis' who 'custodiet', to the *head*keeper himself. The panopticon is to be contracted out by its designers to a free entrepreneur, to a bidder who would see the best opportunity to turn the hands of the inmates to the output of marketable products, and hence the panopticon itself into a profitable enterprise. The head-keeper-contractor would then have his own interest to follow; and his interest would tell him to take care that the inmates remain healthy and strong, that they don't shirk regular labour, that they acquire working habits and thus are gradually reformed, if reform was the reason for their confinement. Once such an interest is in operation, little if any control is necessary. One can rely on the contractor to use the panopticon for the purpose for which it has been designed. One can rely on his desire for profit and his fear of loss to motivate him for the right type of action — that is, the type required to set the panopticon in motion, and in motion in the proper direction. This high-level guardian will be securely guarded by his own calculation. Reason will instruct him that his personal interest demands that the purpose of the panopticon be fully and constantly met.

It can also be safely left to the interest of the contractor to decide how the panopticon ought to be used for its purposes to be met most fully and most securely. To the contractor's question 'What trades may I put my men to when I got them?' Bentham suggests a curt and clear answer: 'Any whatever that you can persuade them to turn their hands to'.[7] And so with all other questions the contractor may deem necessary to ask. Having designed the panopticon and thus assured the general conditions for *a* work to be done successfully — both efficiently and effectively — the designers now pass the buck to the contractor. The designers are themselves urged to withdraw from the scene completely and avoid all temptation of any further meddling with the daily work of their creation. Telling the contractor what to do can add nothing useful to the winning combination of the architecturally determined logic of the panopticon and the profit-oriented calculations of the contractor; it may only put a wedge between the two, and thus detract from the combination's intrinsic potential. All law which is aimed at 'preventing men from following the trades they could get most by' is harmful and should be avoided under all circumstances. 'I would beg that law might be banished from within my walls', says Bentham in the name of the future contractor. And he says it not merely for the sake of the contractor's private gain but also (the two are inseparable) for the sake of the success of the panopticon as the factory of social order. This is exactly what makes freedom of the contractor so uniquely desirable, so infinitely more *socially* useful than the rule by law-bound, dependent functionaries:

> Adopt the contract-plan — regulations in this view are a nuisance: be there ever so few of them, there will be too many. Reject it — be there ever so many of them, they will be too few.[8]

> Power and inclination beget action: unite them — the end is accomplished, the business done.[9]

In his admirably perceptive and insightful study of the criminal law and practice in England at the threshold of the Industrial Revolution, Michael Ignatieff wrote of the 'two personae' of Bentham — the advocate of parliamentary reform and the publicist for the panopticon — as being 'not contradictory, but complementary'.

> The extension of rights within civil society had to be compensated for by the abolition of the tacit liberties enjoyed by prisoners and criminals under the *ancien régime*. In an unequal and increasingly divided society, this was the only way to extend liberty and fortify consent without comprising security.[10]

The contradiction between the totally heteronomous, machine-like existence of the inmates on one extreme, and totally free, unfettered and uninterfered-with condition of the headkeeper-contractor-entrepreneur on the other, with the inspectors (in their dual identity as the servant functionaries of the headkeeper and the masters of the inmates) in between, could not be deeper. Yet this contradiction was in no way an awkward result of an internally inconsistent set of principles; neither was it a logical blunder. Unlike many a philosopher of liberty, human rights or the human condition in general, trying hard to explain (or to legislate about) society in terms of one universal 'essence' of the human species as a whole and every individual in particular, Bentham was fully aware that the purpose of securing the safety and the smooth reproduction of social order cannot but sediment two sharply opposed yet mutually conditioning and validating social modalities: one having a total freedom as its ideal horizon, another striving towards total dependence. The panopticon was not a device confined to the second pole of that opposition; it was not a contraption designed to dispose of the waste produced by the extension of civil and political rights which Bentham preached in the second of his two personae. With a modicum of effort one can read the *Panopticon* as a parable for *the society at large* — a viable society, an orderly society, a society without crime and with non-cooperation easily spotted and dealt with, a society which seeks actively the highest benefit and greatest happiness of its members, a society complete with all functions and roles indispensable for its survival and success. In such a society, the *Panopticon* demonstrates, the freedom of some makes the dependence of others both necessary and profitable; while the unfreedom of one part makes the freedom of another possible. The panopticon is not a supplement to the parliamentary reform; it incorporates the latter as its own condition and legitimation.

Far from being a miscreant of the otherworldly insularity of the panopticon, the free headkeeper-contractor is a character borrowed by Bentham, openly and with pride, from daily life. 'I should have for my contractor — a man who, being engaged in some sort of business that was easy to learn, and doing pretty well with as many hands as he was able to get upon the ordinary terms, might hope to do better still with a greater number, whom he could get upon much better terms.'[11] Men freely pursuing their profits, and while doing so acquiring the ability to command and regulate the labour of others, are born all around in ever greater numbers. The panopticon is not a specialized crime-fighting institution which demands of its head the acquisition of new skills or the transformation of old ones. It is on the contrary an opportunity to do what 'men engaged in business are doing pretty well', only do it better still, under conditions consciously designed for the purpose and hence expected to produce higher returns on the same investment of effort.

Neither are the inmates of the panopticon creatures from outer space, or even a special, criminal category of humans, calling for custom-made rules. As painted by Bentham, their picture is all-too-familiar. One has no difficulty in recognizing the likeness of the 'factory hand'. It is the image of the latter, of the normal springs of his behaviour, of the motives which make him stretch himself and of those which make him stay idle, of the supposed need for a properly organized environment which selects *for* the 'factory hand'

the kind of conduct the factory hand *himself* is apparently incapable
of choosing — which supplies the inspiration for the picture. The
inmate has all those traits the image of the factory hand contains,
and the purpose of the panopticon is once again the provision of
perfect conditions for the best use of the human strengths and
frailties already present in the people currently confined within its
walls. 'Supposing no sage regulations made by any body to nail
them to this or that sort of work, the work they would naturally fall
upon under the hands of a contractor would be that, whatever it
might be, by which there was most money to be made; for the more
the prisoner-workman got, the more the master could get out of
him.'[11]

Thus the *Panopticon* can be read as a descriptive model of the
total society; a miniature model, confined within one rotary
building, but most importantly a corrected model, an improved
model, an idealized model of a 'perfect' society. A society which,
unlike the imperfect original, is neither over- nor under-regulated,
as it locates the regimenting zeal in the sites where it is needed, and
bars it from others; a society which consequently eliminates crime,
contains socially harmful behaviour, eliminates industrial waste; a
society which carefully classifies its members into categories
recognized as different and hence offered differing measures of
freedom and unfreedom which best suit the smooth working of the
whole, and hence everybody's happiness; a society which, thanks to
all that, provides every member with a regular, secure, unthreatening environment for the kind of action to which each member is best
suited.

In its ambition (whether overt or hidden), though not in its scope
and assumed modesty, *Panopticon* may be compared to Parsons's
laboriously erected model of the social system. What both works
seek is nothing less than a model of well-balanced, equilibrated,
cohesive human cohabitation, adaptable to changing tasks, capable
of reproducing the conditions of its own existence, producing
maximum output (however measured) and minimum waste. The
two idealized images are informed by a single purpose. And yet they
propose to reach the purpose following utterly different routes.

Once *Panopticon* is read alongside Parsons's model, pride of
place among the admittedly numerous differences is captured and
kept firmly by one feature of Bentham's controlling machine; or,
rather, by the absence of the feature which figures most promi-
nently in Parsons's model. Absent is the feature variously referred

to as moral education, cultural integration, consensus, value-cluster, 'principal coordination', legitimation, or whatever other names Parsons and his followers used to denote the essentially 'spiritual', normative, rational-emotional nature of societal integration. Between the various levels of the mini-society of the panopticon, silent gaze takes the place of communication; manipulation of the environment, of rewards and of sanctions makes cultural crusades and ideological pressures redundant. The solidity of this mini-society is not forged of legitimation or consensus. It will last, whatever happens to the latter.

Indeed, there is little in the way of culture which unites the strata of Bentham's society, apart from the universal human preference for pleasure rather than pain (or, to be more exact, for the absence rather than presence of pain). This preference, not being a result of training or persuasion, can hardly be considered a cultural trait. It appears in the description of the panopticon as a condition rather than a product; it does not result from the working of the system, being instead the very underlying factor which makes this working possible. This universal human feature is not of human creation; simply, it is the way human beings are. Apart from this one uniting feature, itself of a doubtful cultural provenance, one would search in vain for that common set of cultural norms which Parsons would have us believe is the indispensable requisite of any well-integrated system.

Neither is there any attempt on the part of the 'centre' to convert the 'periphery' to its values; to preach, educate, proselytize. The one belief they seek to inculcate into the minds of their subordinates is the permanence and irrevocability of the rulers' superiority and the ensuing identity of self-interest with unconditional surrender. Otherwise the site which various categories of actors occupy within the system calls for different kinds of behaviour. For one of those categories entirely, for another partly, the required behaviour is generated by the sort of control under which they are placed, rather than by the moral precepts or injunctions, the cultural norms and beliefs or the standards of evaluation and choice they accept. Indeed, little as we know about the working of their minds, it is not less than our understanding of the working of the system demands.

It is the difference, not similarity, which integrates Bentham's system. The perfectly coordinated mini-society is held together by a strictly observed division of power. The division of power, in its turn, consists of nothing more than the distinction between a choice unrestrained and a choice reduced to the bare existential minimum; the distinction between freedom and unfreedom. Those who rule are free; those who are free, rule. Those who are ruled, are unfree; those who are unfree, are ruled.

At the start of his life-long search for the ultimate theory of society, Talcott Parsons expressed his disaffection with the extant concepts of human action, all blind to the inner ambiguity of acting-in-society. Parsons declared his own aim: he wanted a theory of action which would put paid to the traditional weaknesses of its predecessors by accounting, simultaneously, for the voluntary nature *and* non-random character of action. Such a combination of apparently irreconcilable traits was, so Parsons assumed, an irremovable feature of *all* action, a phenomenological 'essence' of the actor's condition. Given this logical incongruence within every single act, this duality being a transcendental, *a priori* truth of every action, Parsons believed the single act in its generalized form ('an action as such') to be the right starting-point for theorizing about society. And this is what he did. Gradually, he built a model of the social system in which every actor shares in the same universal essence: he is freely choosing, while at the same time his actions are de-randomized by the shared cultural system and by societally distributed (and differentiated) roles. Much as all the actors represent the same transcendental duality of action, the way in which the *a priori* proclivities of the actor and the cultural system and social structure interfere (to produce empirically given be-havioural results) are the same for all actors. Parsons's general theory of society is a theory of totality composed of basically identical units.

Selecting the actor and his action as the starting-point for sociological theorizing, and postulating the essential homogeneity of actors, condition and validate each other; one renders the other simultaneously plausible and necessary. That this is the case can be shown not only through logical analysis but demonstrated through a survey of most of sociological theory. The combination of the assumption of actors' homogeneity (the 'actor as such' approach) with the decision to select the social action as the take-off point for a theory of society (sometimes its entire territory) has been in no way confined to Parsons; it is shared by Parsons with his most outspoken critics, for instance ethnomethodologists and by all post-Schutzian theorizing, together with hermeneutically or Wittgenstein-inspired branches of contemporary theory. All these varieties of sociological theory require the concept of a free-choosing agent as an essential unit of society. Members of society being such agents, they all have access to the stock of knowledge at hand; they all shift between various finite provinces of meaning; they all decide upon their respective relevances, typify, use language, produce and decode meanings, and so on. Whatever is necessary for the conduct of daily life is shared by all the actors. Whatever interaction follows is the work of essentially similar and equally equipped members.

Difference, and not similarity, is the starting assumption of Bentham's model. Some actors are freer than others: discrimination in the degree of freedom allotted to various categories of actors is the very stuff of which the social system is moulded. Discrimination preceeds action. The content and the potential of action depend on the place it occupies in the network of interaction, in which those who are free to choose limit the choice of those who are placed at the receiving end. Instead of being an unanticipated outcome of the interplay between 'phenomenologically equal', similarly free agents, social order is something which some people set for others. Within the social order, sites differ in the degree of freedom they offer to, and require from, their incumbents. If it is true that 'men make society', it is also true that some men make the kind of society in which other men must live and act. Some people set norms, some other people follow them.

Drawing his inspiration from cybernetical system-analysis, Michel Crozier linked power inside any organized social network to control over the sources of uncertainty; those closest to the seats of uncertainty (those whose conduct *is* the source of uncertainty in the situation of the others), rule.[12] Action may generate uncertainty in so far as it is free from normative (legal or customary) regulation; the absence or paucity of norms renders conduct poorly predictable, and hence those affected by the conduct in question are exposed to the vagaries of will of those who may choose freely. On the other hand, people may disregard the behaviour of those participants of interaction who are normatively bound and hence behave routinely, in an easily anticipated way: repetitive, monotonous behaviour does not constitute the 'unknown' value in the situational equation and could be relegated to the realm of safe assumptions.

In the light of this analysis, freedom appears as the capacity to rule; as a bid for power. Freedom is power, in so far as there are others who are bound.

As if anticipating the cybernetical insight, Bentham constructed his model of a smoothly functioning, viable and effective system using the differentiation of freedom as his major building block. Bentham's system consists of relational contexts of interactions, not of single roles assigned to single actors, as in Parsons's and similar models. In this system, the whole attention of the architect is focused on rendering the conduct of one part all but transparent to the other (literally, by opening it to the latter's constant scrutiny; indirectly, by forcing it into a range containing little, if any, choice), and rendering the conduct of the other part as opaque to the first as possible (through the device of 'seeing without being seen'; and through virtually removing all constraint from the other part's freedom of choice). Through the opposition between transparency and opacity — or, to put it in more general terms, predictability (certainty) and unpredictability (uncertainty) — the relationship of power and subordination is made secure. Groups of clearly conflicting predispositions and interests are integrated into a harmonious system without any reduction in the scope or intensity of the conflict itself.

Regarding those located in the ambiguous middle range between the poles of the opposition, Bentham asks the sacramental question, 'Quis custodiet ipsos custodies?' He stops short of asking it regarding the guardian of the guardians, the headkeeper-contractor-entrepreneur himself. Indeed, he admits that the law-conscious prospective opponents of the panopticon will consider the question indiscriminately relevant from the bottom to the top of the structure. And so he anticipates the question being addressed to the headkeeper — but only to dismiss it as misdirected. The necessity of meticulous regulation, infinite precautions, carefully directed pressures of environment — which Bentham so keenly pursued when considering the optimal setting for the inmates — is flatly denied in relation to the headkeeper. At this level of the system it may bring nothing but harm. It will certainly detract from the effectiveness of the headkeeper's rule over his wards; but it will also dent the dedication, inventiveness and energy of the head-keeper, and with that the adaptability and the success of the system as a whole.

The headkeeper does not need legal norms and regulations, as he has the right motives for action *and* adequate resources to act upon them. When both are present, the resulting conduct can be *self*-controlled. Monitored by the actor, checked against its results and duly corrected, it will veer towards the desirable pattern. Making profit will be the motive; acting upon it means making saleable products and selling them on the market. Making profit will be a sign of being on the right track. Making a loss will serve as a warning signal that the action should be altered. Gain needs resources; the headkeeper has such resources; hence he can be a free agent and engage in interaction with other free agents on his own initiative and responsibility. Legislators may rest here. From now on they are not needed.

From *now* on. This 'now' has been reached once the properly devised social system has been set in operation. But the legislators may rest because the job of designing has been well done and the system *can afford* to set free some of its members, and *needs* the freedom of some of its members for its own success.

People who theorize models of society are intellectuals — on the whole distinguished members, yet members nevertheless, of the knowledge class (the class of people who 'deal with the production and distribution of symbolic knowledge'[13]). As intellectuals, they are engaged in a specific kind of productive practice which constitutes the mode of existence, a position in relation to the rest of society, an understanding of their own role, and a set of ambitions (an idealized image of that role) entirely of their own. It is these practices, perspectives and ambitions which are processed and theorized into model images of society.[14] Rarely do they appear in social theories without disguise; normally, they are 'ploughed into' the ostensibly objective image, painted in a way which defies an easy determination of the vantage-point from which the picture was seen. They have to be retrieved from the image through a kind of 'sociological hermeneutics', a systematic effort to relate the images to certain known situations and actions of the social category of the image-producers; such an effort, if successful, will allow us to understand the images as projections of specific collective experience.

As spokesmen for the knowledge class — by the logic of their social location, if not by deliberate choice — the intellectuals would tend to regard the social totality in such a way as to render their own mode of work and life central to the functioning of the society; indeed, the theoretical models they produce would tend to represent society as a social totality seen from the vantage-point of the tasks undertaken and postulated by the knowledge class. The nature of such tasks, and hence the vantage-point and the resulting image, would change, along with the historical transformation of the social location and functions of their intellectual actors; they would also vary with the social setting in which the sectors of intellectuals concerned are situated and operate.

According to this rule, the models produced by intellectuals located in academic settings will on the whole display a bias towards symbolic activities. More often than not they will represent society as a series of symbol-management tasks, and conceive of a well-equilibrated society as one in which the domination of certain symbolically articulated values and norms is assured, and their flow and progressive specification is coordinated with societal subdivisions and the differentiation of functions. The remarkable influence and popularity of the Parsonian model were due at least in part to its 'perfect fit' with this setting-generated collective tendency of *academia*. Through the same tendency one can explain the remarkable fact that whatever faults the academic critics found in the once all-powerful Parsonian system, they all further emphasized the centrality of symbol-production and symbol-distribution. With the self-confidence of 'modernity' collapsing and the pluralist eclecticism of 'post-modernity' on the ascendance, they replaced 'central clusters', 'value hierarchies' and 'principal coordinations' with a free-wheeling, scattered, uncoordinated value- and meaning-production — yet never did they question the ultimate assumption of Parsons's vision: that social order is an outcome of the manipulation of symbols.

Against this long-term tendency of academic theorizing, Bentham's model looks remarkably different. Perhaps one can better understand the difference if one remembers that Bentham was not — at least not primarily — a member of the university world. He belonged to a circle of intellectuals living in close proximity to the world of politicians, governmental administrators and social reformers, and engaged in a constant discourse with this world, sharing to a large extent its concerns and worries, its articulation of the tasks at hand, its selection of instruments of societal action and the resources such an action can rely on. No wonder that in the social system as it emerges from Bentham's writings academia, or the intellectuals in their most 'commonsensically obvious', teaching-preaching role, is almost invisible. Which does not mean, however, that the intellectuals — the best of the 'knowledge class' — are missing from the final picture. They are indeed present, and perhaps more formidably still than in the academically produced models — though, like the panopticon inspectors, they 'see without being seen'.

Bentham's model is construed from the vantage-point of intellectuals as designers, as *expert* owners of knowledge of the laws which guide human conduct and of the skills needed to build social settings within which such laws can be turned to the best advantage. The perfectly equilibrated world of the panopticon is a contrived, designed world; the product of a knowledgeable, thoughtful, rational architect. The politicians are builders guided by his drawings. Neither the intellectual-designer nor the politicians are needed once the construction is complete. A social system which needs free entrepreneurs and offers ideal conditions to exercise their freedom for the common benefit can operate on its own and self-perpetuate itself without the day-to-day interference of busy-body blueprint-makers, and without the vigilance of moral preachers and teachers of social virtues. But when all this began, the design already was.

In both types of models discussed here the intellectuals appear as 'legislators', those who determine the 'norm' for well-integrated, viable social systems. They can perform the legislators role, however, in at least two different ways: as *symbol-operators*, ideologists — as in models of Parsons's type; or as *expert designers*, technologists — as in Bentham's or similar models. In the first case, the cognitive perspective prompts the model-constructors to perceive of freedom as a feature or a right of the 'individual as such'; as a universal attribute of all units of the system, made uniform by their shared condition as objects of education, socialization or cultural training in general. In the second case, freedom appears as a factor in the mechanism of production and reproduction of the social order; as such, it is located in the strategically crucial knots which hold the web together. It remains a judiciously allocated resource, always considered in a distributional context — as one end of a relationship the second end of which is heteronomy. Freedom is here generated by such a relationship, being at the same time the paramount condition of its perpetuation. Freedom is privilege and power.

On the Sociogenesis
of Freedom

There are some contemporary meanings of 'freedom' in which all humans are inescapably free, even if they do not know about it, do not think of it or flatly deny it when asked. Humans are fundamentally free as agents who act rather than abstain from action, or refrain from acting rather than act in a certain way. Here 'freedom' is just another way of stating the obvious, that there is always more than one logically possible way of acting — a trivial truth, tautologically contained in the very idea of 'action'. Or humans are fundamentally free as the bearers of responsibility for the consequences of their conduct; an understanding of freedom which is derivative of some religiously founded moral beliefs or legal constructs. Or, more philosophically, humans are fundamentally free as their life can be nothing else but their own project, an 'in order to', future-oriented activity — even if more often that not this life is perceived by them as a series of surrenders to necessities, and is interpreted in 'because of' terms, as something determined by the past. Sometimes freedom is revealed as a universal property of humans: all instances of heteronomous conduct and external constraints are peeled away as so many superfluous artifices. Sociologically, such interpretations of 'freedom' are uninteresting as they eliminate from vision the fact that freedom is itself a social fact, socially produced and socially endowed with the meaning it happens to carry at a particular time or place. From a sociological point of view, such interpretations should be seen as objects of sociology-of-knowledge inquiry, or of sociological hermeneutics, rather than as hypotheses about reality to be tested for their truth.

Most of the books with 'Freedom' in the title or subtitle focus on such and similar meanings of the term. By and large they attempt to reconstruct, reinterpret and critically assess influential intellectual writings on the subject. They are part of the ongoing philosophical discourse through which 'freedom' as an idea, a value, a 'utopian horizon' of our civilization, is kept alive while being reassessed by successive generations. These books, so to speak, belong to a philosophy which exists solely as its own history.

The books in question carry great cultural importance, being a part of the discourse which they record and in the continuation of which they are an indispensable condition. Their other significance, which their scientifically oriented authors often claim, is not, however, unquestionable. As *history* books they are expected to untangle the inner logic of the phenomenon they study, present its later forms as the outcome of the earlier ones and reveal the forces responsible for the passage from one form to another. To do all this they ought to select from the complex and wide-ranging realities of the past a subset more or less complete and self-sustained, that is a subset containing all the factors needed to account for the known transformations of the phenomenon under study. In most cases, however, the subset selected is that of the ideas themselves. It is suggested then, overtly or obliquely, that the successive trans-formations of the phenomenon called 'freedom' are identical with successive conceptualizations of it. The history of freedom consists then of a series of reformulations, redefinitions, recapitulations, as well as intellectual discoveries or inventions. Ideas are born of ideas, crossfertilize with ideas, beget other ideas. It can be seen that the writers of the books in question project upon the topic they study the experience of the form of life they collectively practise; or rather, its counterfactual assumptions — the supposition that the ideas themselves, their inner strengths or weaknesses, their cohe-sion or incoherence, decide their acceptance or rejection. As a result, they write the history of freedom as a history of their fellow-intellectuals.

Yet the importance of intellectual formulations of freedom has always derived from the fact that they grappled with real problems of their time; concepts extant in the continuing discourse were used to articulate the experience of new social structures and processes, to render the change meaningful, and it was in this use that they changed themselves and their meanings. All the significance the history of intellectual work had for the history of society at large was due to the fact that it was not an incestuous affair of professional thinkers.

'Sociogenesis' (a term borrowed, with gratitude, from Norbert

Elias) of freedom refers to those departures and dislocations in social figurations, large and small, which led to the successive modifications in the network of dependencies and hence also in the contexts of human interaction, and which the discourse of freedom articulated. It is assumed that every such dislocation created social tensions appearing to contemporaries as an unresolved social problem, either demanding the rejection of past concepts or their innovative use. The apparent unity of discourse over time, an illusion generated by the 'history of ideas' approach, dissipates into a series of discontinuities, only partly disguised by the institutionalized historical memory. What is revealed then is that rather than a gradual unfolding of the full meaning of the idea from its original embryonic form, the history of freedom is a bridge spanning a wide range of social figurations, with their specific conflicts and power struggles.

Perhaps the oldest idea of freedom referred to an act rather than a condition: a decision of the powerful to release someone subject to their power from slavery, captivity or bondage. Such a release — manumission (from *manumittere*, to send forth from one's hand) — was for all practical intents and purposes an act of 'humanization': in classical antiquity slaves or captives were seen and legally treated as chattels alongside the rest of their master's property; damaging or destroying them counted as perpetrating an assault on the master's estate rather than on 'human rights' — and the damage had to be repaired, just as in the case of stolen sheep or a burnt shed. Manumission transformed a slave or a bondsman into the freedman, in most cases not fully a human being but not a chattel either. The freedman — *libertinus* — bore the mark of his former state, a mark impossible to wash out, sometimes up to the third generation. His was a wholly negative status; he was *not* a slave. To make sense his status had to be measured against the state of slavery or bondage. The latter showed who he was, while the status of a person who was never a slave offered little guidance as to his social situation. Whatever 'freedom' there was in the identity of the freedman, was relational. It referred to what he had already ceased to be and what some others still remained. It referred also to a third agent, the only true agent in the triangle, as it were — that power which made the distinction. Freedmen had to be *made* free. Liberation was not itself an act of freedom.

It can be argued that the theory and practice of heteronomy, or the negativity of freedom, bequeathed by Judaic as much as

Graeco-Roman antiquity, shed some light on the notorious 'Pelagian heresy' episode in the early history of the Church. The teaching of Pelagius, and the vehement response it solicited from St Augustine (later to be repeated virtually intact by St Thomas Aquinas and John Calvin, though never officially accepted as the canon of the Church) were concerned with the origin and the scope of 'free will'. According to Pelagius, God *made* humans free; having been so made, humans could choose between good and evil according to their will. It was up to them to live towards salvation or doom; having been made free, having been given the gift of free will, they bore entire and sole responsibillity for their deeds. The teaching of Pelagius seems to agree with the practice of antiquity: manumission was indeed the end of the state of slavery, and among other things it meant the assumption by the freedman of the full responsibility for his conduct. True, in numerous cases there was a condition attached to the act of liberation; *libertini* could be obliged to remain in the service of their former master, or perform various duties towards him. The very act of manumission could be conditional on the regular and perpetual performance of such duties, and rescinded in the case of failure to do so. But even that eventuality bore witness to the fact that the freedman was now a 'bearer of responsibility'; he could choose to be loyal or to betray his master, and should be rewarded or punished for his choice accordingly. Antiquity knew, however, an unconditional and irreversible liberation as well. In such cases the master, who exercised his power at the beginning — in the act of manumission — resigned his dominion over the former slave for the future.

It is likely that precisely this consequence of the act of liberation rendered the teaching of Pelagius unacceptable to St Augustine and the powers that be who stood behind him. Indeed, Pelagius reduced the Church to an association of moral preachers, and refused it all other power over the faithful but that of a spiritual exhortation. If it is true that in his omnipotence God endowed humans with an irrevocable gift of free will, by the same token He put their fate in their own hands and decided to renounce all power over their conduct. By proxy, His decision would have cast doubt over the claims of the Church to all practical control over its flock, and bode ill for the status of the emerging ecclesiastic hierarchy. It was this threat which St Augustine set to ward off with his complex and notoriously ambivalent doctrine of divine grace and original sin. According to this doctrine, humans forever continue to bear the mark of their culpable and reprehensible past — much like freedmen carry to their death, and to the death of their offspring, the stigma of their original slavery. All humans participate in the original sin — the act of rejection of God's custody and the divine order. Hence their innate propensity to put evil over good. The fact that they cannot propagate their earthly existence but through carnal desire and sexual passions testifies to the lasting rule of bodily matter (evil) over spirit (good). In this sense they remain slaves. Their freedom is confined to the choice of evil; choosing good may be only the work of divine grace. Humans need the continuous rule of their divine master: they need to be watched, censored, admonished, forced onto the road to virtue. By proxy again, the Church, this collective vicar of God on earth, is entitled to watch, to censure and to enforce virtue. (It could be of some sociological interest to note that it was not the Church which finally rejected the teaching of Pelagius; while the pope Zosimus remained in two minds as to the wisdom of condemning the Pelagian doctrine, the emperor Honorius outlawed the hapless advocate of free will, and the Church followed suit.)

The episode of Pelagian heresy reveals a new, important aspect of freedom. Perhaps for the first time a theory appears which casts freedom fairly and squarely on the side of evil, only to employ it as a justification of heteronomous rule. This theory accords well with the social conditions of the centuries to follow, conditions under which no human being could reasonably claim to be 'complete in himself', self-sufficient, in full mastery over the circumstances of his life or over the resources his life-business required; conditions which had no room for 'masterless men' and made the lack of attachment, of vassalage or corporate membership (vagrancy, vagabondage) into the most terrifying of social dangers and most odious of crimes. In the centuries to follow, up to the dawn of modern times, society knew of no other method of preserving social order and no other vehicle of control than the rule of the master or of the local or occupational corporation. Or, rather, it relied unknowingly and unthinkingly on such methods and vehicles for its familiar and hence unthreatening way of life. No wonder the sight of a masterless or non-belonging person tended to generate that anxiety which the bringing into relief of the heretofore tacit assumptions of social existence must produce. The condition of being masterless must have been doubly alarming, as it were: firstly on account of the difficulty of controlling it and, second, as it presented social order as something which must be consciously taken care of and will not preserve itself on its own.

Under those circumstances freedom such as may be accommodated without perceived threat to the society is always something granted, and through its origin in the act of granting something (at least in principle) tightly controlled. In addition, such freedom is always partial, 'in certain respects'; either it consists in exemption from clearly defined, specific obligations or jurisdiction, or in the membership of a collectivity sharing in a privilege. Freedom is indeed a privilege, and a privilege offered sparingly and on the whole without enthusiasm on the side of the givers.

In the Middle Ages freedom was clearly related to the power struggle. Freedom meant exemption from some aspects of superior power; free status testified to the strength of those who won it, and the weakness of those who reluctantly had to concede it. Magna Carta Libertatum, arguably the most symbolic and famous document of that struggle, was a joint product of the doubtful dynastic entitlements of King John, the high costs of the Crusades, which stretched to breaking-point the resources and patience of the king's baronial subjects, the need to mobilize the knights for military service and the growing threat of civil war. Magna Carta — the 'great charter of freedom' — was forced upon a monarch lacking the strength to resist it. It acceded a series of 'freedoms' which the barons were from then on to enjoy and the king promised not to infringe; among those freedoms, security against 'arbitrary' (i.e. not agreed upon) taxes loomed large. The charter legalized the status of the 'freeman' and indirectly defined it as one which precludes imprisonment or dispossession except by the judgement of peers (other freemen) and the law of the land.

Magna Carta, therefore, transformed the temporary weakness of the monarchy into the law; it subjected the actions of the monarch to permanent constraint, rendering them thereby more predictable to the king's subjects, and depriving them of much of the 'source of uncertainty' character. Merely legal constraints were obviously not yet trusted, as in the text of the Charter the barons had written their right to take up arms against the king if he should violate the limits of his power; for the freemen, defence of their freedom, even by force, became one of the moves sanctioned by the rules of the game — now part of the political order and not its violation. With the right to resistance, barons turned themselves into a permanent 'uncertainty factor' in the situation of the monarch and by the same token put effective constraints on the king's freedom. Indirectly, the limits imposed now upon the actions of the monarch affecting the status of his free subjects defined the notion of 'arbitrary', or 'despotic', rule as a specific 'royal crime' — a transgression of social order which monarchs are inclined to commit and for which they ought to be punished.

Freedom was, therefore, a privilege won from the king by a relatively narrow category of wealthy and powerful subjects; soon the name of 'freeman' came to be used synonymically with the concept of a person of noble birth and breeding. 'Free' were those of the king's subjects over whom the king enjoyed only a limited jurisdiction.

In the late Middle Ages (starting, in fact, from the twelfth century), the privilege of freedom came to be granted not just to individual persons or family lineages but to whole corporations, particularly to the towns. Freedom of a town could mean an exemption from tax or other financial burdens; the removal of restrictions and regulations imposed upon trade; the right to self-government; and a host of ostensibly insignificant or petty privileges, which however played an important ceremonial and symbolic role, re-enacting the town's autonomy from landed property and the monarchy itself. The town's freedom involved the right to bestow the 'freedom of the town' upon selected — usually the wealthiest — citizens. Being a freeman of a given city meant the enjoyment of certain immunities from the city power on top of sharing in the corporative privileges of the city.

In the freedom of the city, the most seminal factor, of immeasurable historical consequence, was the exemption of the city and its many trades from the jurisdiction of the land estate. The freedom of the cities marked and conditioned the progressive split of wealth into two separate categories, each subject to its own rules: with one of the two categories winning its independence from another only to submit it in the end, after centuries of struggle, to its power. In the words of Louis Dumont:

> In the traditional type of society, immovable wealth (estates) is sharply distinguished from the movable wealth (money, chattels) by the fact that rights in land are enmeshed in the social organisation in such a manner that superior rights accompany power over men. Such rights or 'wealth', appearing essentially as a matter of relations between men, are intrinsically superior to movable wealth. . . . With the moderns, a revolution occurred in this respect: the link between

> immovable wealth and power over men was broken, and movable
> wealth became fully autonomous in itself, as the superior aspect of
> wealth in general. . . . It should be noted that it is only at this point
> that a clear distinction can be drawn between what we call 'political'
> and . . . 'economic'[1]

The emancipation of 'free towns' from the powers of the local
barons broke the most important link between wealth and rights
over people. The freedom of towns meant in practice the separation
of the circulation of money and commodities from the traditional
structures of social organization, and in particular from the network
of mutual rights and obligations surrounding the hierarchical
ownership of land and participation in the land's produce. Inside
the city walls the creation and distribution of wealth could develop
unconstrained by traditional relations of power — relations experienced as 'natural', as an integral part of the 'great chain of being' (to
employ Arthur Lovejoy's famous expression). The freedom of the
towns meant, therefore, the gestation of economy as a system of
human actions and relations separate from 'polity' and the whole
universe of traditional rights over people; a system which tends to
become a 'whole' in its own right, a self-contained and self-
regulating totality, kept in motion and on course solely by the
impersonal logic of supply, demand and circulation of goods (the
'invisible hand' of Adam Smith, which forged the common weal out
of the multitude of disparate, self-interested actions of individuals,
coordinated by nothing but market exchange of their assets). More
generally still, the freedom of the towns — having cut urban life
away from the world in which human dependencies had been
enmeshed in land property and hence perceived as 'natural' —
provided the foundation of the typically modern 'artificialism': the
conception of the social order not as a natural condition of
mankind, but as a product of human wit and administration, as
something which ought to be designed and implemented in a way
dictated by human reason and aimed against precisely the 'natural'
(morally ugly, irrational and disorderly) predispositions of the
human animals. City life separated men from nature; the freedom
of the towns separated men from the 'laws of nature' — the
submission of the business of life to the rhythm and the vagaries of
phenomena on which human wills and skills had little, if any, effect.

It has been clear from this perfunctory survey of the uses of
freedom in ancient and medieval times that freedom is in no way a
modern invention; neither the institutionalized relations which

provided for a degree of individual autonomy (or, to see it from the other end, for a limitation of power prerogatives), nor the concepts which articulated them, have been confined to the modern era. Moreover, it was in the Middle Ages that the hothouses were built in which the plants of modern freedoms were propagated. And yet the modern form of freedom differs considerably from its antecedents; a similar name hides, in fact, sharply different qualities.

Libraries have been written on the uniqueness and the many remarkable attributes of the modern (Western) phenomenon of freedom. It seems, however, that from the sociological point of view two of the undoubtedly many distinctive features of modern freedom are of particular interest: its intimate link with individualism, and its genetic and cultural connection with the market economy and capitalism (the type of society most recently defined by Peter L. Berger as 'production for a market by enterprising individuals or combines with the purpose of making a profit'[2]).

The hard core of individualism, as Colin Morris recently commented, 'lies in the psychological experience with which we began: the sense of a clear distinction between my being, and that of other people. The significance of this experience is greatly increased by our belief in the *value* of human beings in themselves'. Once the stamp of special — indeed, supreme — value had been impressed upon the otherwise mundane experience of doing one's things and thinking one's thoughts, an 'acute self-awareness followed' — an impulse to look on one's 'own self' as an object of tender care and cultivation. Such a self-awareness, says Morris, 'has been a distinctive feature of Western man'. More than that, the resulting form of individualism may well be regarded as 'an eccentricity among cultures'.[3]

What is so eccentric, we may add, is not the cultural precept assigning special value (special possibilities, special tasks, special moral duties) to single men as distinct from the group to which they belong. Such precepts could be found among many cultures, indeed long before the phenomenon called 'Western man' appeared in a recognizable form. Dumont found such precepts in ancient Indian theology and religious practices, only to trace them later to quite a few currents of ancient Greek philosophy and, perhaps most importantly, to the teaching of the Christian Church. What, however, united the Indian religion, the philosophies of the Epicureans, Cynics and Stoics and the homilies of the Church Fathers, setting them at the same time apart from the modern individualist philosophies, was the 'other worldliness' of the individual. As far as he was a true individual — that is a free chooser, an autonomous bearer of moral responsibility, a master of his own life — man was placed outside the world of the mundane, daily life, paying for his freedom with the renunciation of social duties and leaving the vainglorious bustle of earthly concerns behind. The individual was therefore an essentially non-social being, or at least someone existing outside society. The road to individuality was hence open to the chosen few only. It led through mystical immersion, philosophical refinement, extreme religious piety. Whoever followed that road had to be prepared to end up as a *sannyasin*, a Diogenes-style philosopher beggar, a pillar saint or a desert anchorite. That was a road for the blessed, the thoughtful or the desperate — certainly not for the hewers of wood and the drawers of water. It was explored by the philosophers and the religious devotees who never thought of the self-estrangement they chose or accepted as a realistic proposition (much less a universal duty) for ordinary mortals. The philosophy of other-worldly individualism was not a formula for proselytizing.

If the other-worldly individuality was a prize waiting at the end of the tortuous and thorny path of righteousness, the modern inner-worldly individuality — one wedded to the unique, modern, mode of freedom — could be, and has been, articulated as a universal attribute of human beings; more than that, as the *most* universal, or rather the most decisive among universal attributes. To Aristotle it seemed natural to begin thinking of human existence from *polis* — a collective entity which gave character and identity to everyone who came within its embrace — thus defining humans as 'political animals', members and participants in the communal life. Yet it seemed natural to Hobbes and other pioneers of modern thought to start from ready-made, pre-social individuals, and from them and their essential, inseparable attributes, to proceed to the question of how such individuals can associate in order to form something so 'supra-individual' as a society or state. The opposition between the two strategies designates the enormous distance separating the modern inner-worldly individuality from its ostensibly other-worldly predecessor, which always resided on the margins of society and its institutions, and in a sense independently from them.

There was, however, another important feature which set modern individuality apart. Having been placed firmly inside mundane social life, it occupied from the very start an ambiguous position towards society, one pregnant with never-subsiding tension. On the one hand, the individual was credited with a capacity for judgement, for recognizing interests and taking decisions on how to act upon them — all qualities which make living together in a society feasible. On the other hand, however, individuality was imbued with intrinsic dangers: the very interestedness of the individual, which prompted him to seek collective guarantees for security, enticed him at the same time to resent the constraints which such guarantees implied. In particular, the safety offered by the supra-individual authority was conditional on the suppression of such aspects of the individual which militated against life in association (and were hence dubbed 'animal drives' or 'passions'). Only when such anti-social attributes are safely disposed of, or kept in check, will human beings become complete, fulsome individuals. Hence the duality of modern individuality: on the one hand, it is the natural, inalienable appurtenance of every human being; on the other hand, however, it is something to be created, trained, legislated upon, enforced by the authorities acting on behalf of the 'common weal' of society as a whole. Let us note immediately that what such an element of artificiality implied was the possibility that not all human beings are equally amenable to the polishing/perfecting treatment and hence not all have an equal chance of becoming individuals in the full sense of the word. In some cases, training may prove inconclusive and enforcement become permanent.

Before we attempt to explore the sociological significance of such an implication, a more fundamental question must be asked. The relatively sudden appearance of the universalistic and inner-worldly concept of individuality is, to think of it, a mystery; all the more so as it took place only in one small area of the world and in one relatively short period of history. It cannot be explained away as the felicitous invention of a philosopher or a philosophical school which happened to capture the imagination of contemporaries: the concept in its many applications, and in the practices it legitimized and inspired, came to light simultaneously in too many social networks and processes to be traced back to a single book or even to a series of books (the possibility of such tracing being an illusion brought about and sustained by the 'history of ideas' perspective). It seems more likely that if the philosophical insight into the earthly autonomy of the human individual reverberated so widely and soon saturated the self-consciousness of an entire historical epoch, it was because it resonated so well with a new kind of social experience —

so new and distinct that it could no longer be spoken about and accounted for in terms of estates, communities or corporations. It seems likely that this novel experience contains the key to our mystery.

This novel experience, contrary to popular and simplified accounts, did not consist in a sudden weakening, much less a disappearance, of social dependence — the degree to which human beings were moulded, instructed, controlled, evaluated, censored, 'kept in line' and if necessary 'brought back into the fold' by fellow-members of society. The degree of social dependence so understood remains by and large stable through the ages, being an indispensible condition of the existence and perpetuation of human society. There are no human beings outside society, however much they depend on resources they personally command for their survival, and however independent in the decisions they feel. It was, rather, the way in which social pressures had been exercised which underwent a profound change, and resulted in the experience of being left, ultimately, to one's own discretion and choice. The change consisted first and foremost in the replacement of a unified, unchallenged and easily placeable source of authority by a plethora of partial, mutually unrelated, sometimes mutually contradictory authorities, all behaving as if other authorities did not exist, and all demanding the impossible: sole loyalty to themselves. Social necessity now spoke in many voices, which together sounded more like a cacophony than a chorus. It was largely left to the listener to extricate from the noise a consistent tune to follow. To an extent voices cancelled each other out; no one voice was able to secure a clear and indisputable superiority for the motif it developed. This had a double effect on the 'listener': on the one hand, he was granted a new authority of arbitration; on the other, he was burdened with the new responsibility for the resulting choice.

Neither was that novel experience something which came simultaneously to all denizens of Western Europe, in all countries and at all levels of social hierarchy. As recent studies have convincingly demonstrated, the conditions underlying the emergence of individuality appeared in England well before any other place. D. A. Wrigley documented the high rate of social mobility, the decline of rights and obligations linked to kinship, the unusually large extent of market mediation in the circulation of goods, and the relative weakening of communal authority by an advanced state bureaucracy — which all took place in England centuries before they spread to the continent of Europe.⁴ Alan Macfarlane traced English uniqueness as far back as the thirteenth century and noted that those 'foreigners who visited or read about England, and Englishmen who travelled and lived abroad, could not have escaped noticing that they were moving not merely from one geographical, linguistic, climatic zone to another but to and from a society in which almost every aspect of the culture was diametrically opposed to that of the surrounding nations'.⁵ The differences between countries were, however, those of timing; the differences between levels of social hierarchy proved to be in the long run much more seminal, as they appeared much more resistant to the levelling impact of time.

In fact, individuality was the fate of *some* people; and as in the case of freedom, it was experienced as such in so far as it remained a distinction rather than a universal condition.

This fact has not necessarily been reflected in the philosophical analyses of the concepts of individuality, personal autonomy and freedom. Instead, they have concentrated on the sites where life condition could be articulated as individuality and freedom — and these were selective sites. The unravelling of the experience tied to such sites took the philosophers a long time. Edward Craig distinguished recently three successive themes in the Western (and modern) philosophers' ratiocinations on the human condition.⁶ In early modern times, and particularly at the Age of Enlightenment, the 'similarity thesis' dominated philosophical thought: the intoxicating experience of freshly obtained freedom from external determinants of choice, perceived as a mastery over external reality; a mastery similar — perhaps even equal — to that previously reserved only to God. Soon, however, the inevitable outcome of individual self-determination — the clash of wills, the disparity between individual intentions and factual outcome — was discovered, and the attention of philosophers move to the ubiquitous conflict between moral freedom and physical necessity, individual desires and social requirements; the practical consequences of the clash of wills have been articulated as the reified, indifferent, nature-like solidity and resilience of social reality ('reality' in so far as it could not be wished away). Only towards the end of the nineteenth century did the theme of the 'agency' or 'practice' begin to gain ascendancy, a theme which drew conclusions from both the naïvety of early optimism and the despair which followed its collapse. This latest theme — which ties man's freedom of choice (though not necessarily freedom to achieve intended results) to the inconclusive and hence manipulable character of external determination — comes perhaps closest to the articulation of the most fundamental condition of modern individualism: the pluralism, heterogeneity, dis-ordination of social powers, which creates both the necessity and the possibility of individual choice, subjective motivation and personal responsibility.

By and large, some sociologists had anticipated this relatively recent philosophical conclusion. They dug for the roots of modern individuality in various parts of history or social structure, but they agreed on the essentials: individuality as value, intense pre-occupation with individual distinction and uniqueness, the poignant experience of being a 'self' and 'having' a self at the same time (i.e. being obliged to care, defend, 'keep clean' etc. one's self, much as one is regarding other possessions) are a necessity imposed upon certain classes of people by the social context of their lives, and the most relevant aspect of such context is the absence of an unequivocal and comprehensive norm able to provide (and to enforce) an unambiguous behavioural recipe for the 'life project' as a whole, as well as for the ever-changing situations of daily life. In the absence of one all-powerful, overwhelming current, individual ships must have their own gyroscopes to keep them on course. Such a 'gyroscope' role is performed by the individual capacity to monitor and correct one's own conduct. This capacity is called 'self-control'.

The freedom of the modern individual arises therefore from uncertainty; from a certain 'under-determination' of external reality, from the intrinsic controversiality of social pressures. The free individual of modern times is, to employ Robert Jay Lifton's famous expression,[7] a 'Protean man', namely a person who is simultaneously *under*-socialized (as no all-embracing and unquestionable formula is forthcoming from the world 'out there'), and *over*-socialized (as no 'hard core' in the sense of assigned, inherited or awarded identity is hard enough to withstand the cross-currents of external pressures, and hence the identity must be continuously negotiated, adjusted, constructed without interruption and with no prospect of finality).

The responsibility for such a state of affairs sociologists laid at the door of that disunity, plurality of powers and heterogeneity of culture which is more and more recognized as the most conspicuous characteristic of modern society. Emile Durkheim linked the birth of modern individuality with the growing division of labour and the resulting exposure of each and any member of the society to specialized and uncoordinated areas of authority, none of which may claim a total and comprehensive loyalty. Georg Simmel saw the individual tendency to summon 'the utmost in uniqueness and particularisation' as a necessity of a life which 'is composed more and more' of disparate 'contents and offerings'; the only solid ground the person can hope for (and even this in vain) in the whirlwind of chaotic impressions the modern urban environment never tires of supplying, is his own 'personal identity'.

Norbert Elias's study of modernization as a 'civilizing process' (which put into historical perspective the link between modern society and the civilizing contraints imposed upon 'naturally' violent and passion-ridden human behaviour first brought into relief by Siegmund Freud) presents the experience of the autonomy of the individual, of his 'unrelatedness' to extrinsic dependencies, as an outcome of the process of self-distancing and self-detachment, rather than a reflection of an 'objective' distance and lack of relation. The confused character of external pressures and their evident lack of direction are perceived as the meaninglessness and purposelessness of whatever exists 'outside' the individual. Hence the separation of the thinking, feeling, purpose-setting 'self' from the inert, inanimate objects of his thought and action. Yet this setting-apart is possible (and, arguably, unavoidable) only because interpersonal external compulsions have been already 'incorporated' and reforged in the self-monitoring ego (Freud's 'garrison in the conquered city').

> It is these civilisational self-controls, functioning in part automatically, that are now experienced in individual self-perception as a wall, either between 'subject' and 'object' or between one's own 'self' and other people ('society').

> The notion of individuals deciding, acting, and 'existing' in absolute independence of one another is an artificial product of men which is characteristic of a particular stage in the development of their self-perception. It rests partly on a confusion of ideals and facts, and partly on a reification of individual self-control mechanisms.[8]

If Elias develops the interpretation of modern individuality along the lines first explored by Simmel, another distinguished contemporary sociologist, Niklas Luhmann, follows the line chosen originally by Durkheim. He refers the origins of modern individuality to 'the transition from stratified to functional differentiation within society'; this transition, in its turn, leads 'to greater differentiation of personal and social systems', because 'with the adoption of functional differentiation individual persons can no longer be firmly located in one single subsystem of society, but rather must be regarded a priori as socially displaced'. In simpler words, everyone is in a sense a stranger, a marginal person in one respect or another; not belonging to any 'total' entity but forced to interact with many such entities, 'individuals are all the more provoked into interpreting the difference between themselves and the environment . . . in terms of their own person, whereby the ego becomes the focal point of all their inner experiences and the environment loses most of its contours.'[9]

In Luhmann's view, such relative estrangement of each and every person from each and every 'subsystem' within society opens a wide space for individual development and allows the inner life of the individual to reach a depth and richness never attained under conditions of close communal control. On the other hand, however, mutual estrangement of individuals puts the very continuation of interpersonal communication in doubt; indeed, a meaningful discourse and agreement becomes improbable. For communication to take place in spite of this, the inner experiences of its subjects, organized as it were around separate focal points, must be validated intersubjectively, that is socially. According to Luhmann, such validation is indeed accomplished in modern society through the medium of love: a socially approved and supported medium of communication in which the interacting subjects reciprocally recognize the validity and relevance of each other's inner experience — one partner marking the other's experience as real by taking it as the motive for their own action.

We may observe here that the incertitude which haunts every individual self-synthesis as long as it remains not-yet-socially-confirmed — the condition so penetratingly explored by Luhmann — triggers off an obsessive desire for certainty which can be quenched with means other than 'love'. Bensman and Lilienfeld suggest psychotherapy as one means; they consider the invention of the psychotherapeutic interview to be 'one of the great accomplishments of psychology', 'where the weight of privacy is, for an hour, lifted'[10] and where a scientifically respectable, and hence socially credible, valuation is offered. Andrew J. Weigert generalized the role exemplified by psychiatry, pointing out that the need for 'truth' (i.e. suprapersonally confirmed, authoritative and thus socially valid grounds for one's self-interpretation) 'engages citizens with experts': 'we moderns live a life dominated by the scientific attitude without ourselves being true scientists'[11]; the exclusive right to speak with the authority of scientific, extrapersonal knowledge, has been reserved to the expert specialists. One can think also of other media which successfully meet the demand generated by the validation problems of ego-centred synthesis — such as the consumer industry and its advertising arm, or indeed totalitarian political movements or fundamentalist religious sects. We will return to this topic in more detail in the next chapter.

Apart from its close link with individualism, the modern version of freedom is marked by its intimate relation with capitalism. Indeed, the doubts voiced by the political opponents of capitalism as to whether that is really the case have little chance of winning the argument, as the statement they question is virtually self-confirming. Modern renderings of freedom and definitions of capitalism are articulated in such a way that they presume the necessity of unbreakable connection between the two and make the supposition that one can exist without the other logically flawed, if not absurd.

As Mike Emmison aptly observed,[12] what we call capitalism is a situation where the eternal, substantive economic functions of any human society, namely the satisfaction of human needs through exchange with nature and one's fellows, are implemented through the application of means–ends calculus to the question of choice between scarce and limited resources. But choice and means–ends calculus (namely, motivated, purposeful and reason-monitored behaviour) are the essential, defining characteristics of freedom as understood in modern society. What follows is that capitalism, by its very definition, opens to freedom a huge, if not decisive sphere of social life: the production and the distribution of goods aimed at the satisfaction of human needs. Under the capitalist form of economic organization, freedom (economic freedom, at least) may flourish. More than that, freedom becomes a necessity. Without freedom, the aim of economic activity cannot be fulfilled.

Capitalism provides practical conditions for free-choice be-haviour by 'disembedding' the economic function, that is by cutting economic activity off from all other social institutions and functions. As long as the economy remained 'embedded' (and it remained so to the point of not being conceptually distinguished from social life in general, for the most part of human history — up to the eighteenth century, in fact), productive and distributive activity was subject to pressures of numerous social norms not aimed directly at the activity itself, yet oriented towards the survival and reproduction of other vital institutions. Thus production and distribution were subject to kinship duties, communal loyalties, corporative solidarities, religious rituals or hierarchical stratification of life patterns. Capitalism rendered all such extrinsic norms irrelevant and thus 'liberated' the economic sphere for the unchallenged rule of means–ends calculus and free-choice behaviour. The capitalist economy is not only the territory where freedom may be practised in the least constrained fashion, uninterfered with by any other social pressures or considerations; it is also the nursery where the modern idea of freedom was sown and cultivated, to be later grafted on other branches of increasingly ramified social life. There is a lot of evidence that even in the economic sphere proper the absolute rule of freedom is more a postulate or an ideal than reality; nevertheless, in no other area does freedom come so close to undivided rule as it does in the economy.

Capitalism defines freedom as the ability to guide one's behaviour solely by means–ends calculus, without needing to concern oneself with other considerations ('other' will be, by definition, such considerations as require the use of less efficient means, or compromising the ends, or both). What, however, is the social substance of means–ends calculus?

Philippe Dandi has recently offered a succinct description of what he calls the 'primitive, Western discourse of power': 'We shall conquer and subjugate nature, rule over the laws of physics and *have* power over things. This mentality is also expressed in our desire to treat people in the same way as we have learnt to treat things. We see each other as instruments to mould and manoeuvre as if people also were things'.[13] In behaviour subordinated solely to means–ends calculus, other people are means to an end — much like things which serve the same purpose (raw materials, means of transport, etc.). Behaviour guided by means–ends calculus strives to render other people 'thinglike'; that is, it tends to deprive other people of choice, and by the same token makes them objects rather than subjects of action.

There is therefore an intrinsic ambiguity in freedom in its modern edition, wed to capitalism. The effectiveness of freedom demands that some other people stay unfree. To be free means to be allowed and to be able to keep others unfree. Thus freedom in its modern, economically defined form does not differ from its pre-modern applications in respect of its social-relations content. It is, as before, selective. It may be truly achieved (as distinct from philosophically postulated) only by a part of the society. It constitutes one pole in a relationship which has normative regulation, constraint and coercion as its other pole.

This crucial feature of modern freedom is more often than not concealed in philosophical generalization of an experience limited in fact to the privileged category of people. Self-awareness of mastery over one's conditions (mastery inevitably attained at the expense of somebody else's subordination) is articulated as the collective achievement of mankind; purposeful, efficiency-conscious, reason-guided conduct is identified with rationalization of society as such. In the end, mystifying rather than clarifying statements about the achievements of an unspecified 'man' are made — of which the following is a good example: 'World-mastery, or at least the potential for it, has come to man through rationalisation. Humans have replaced God as the masters of their destiny'.[14] What is left undefined, is whether the 'humans' who replaced God as masters, and the 'humans' whose destiny is mastered, are the same humans.

This confusion is responsible for quite a few persistent misunderstandings which haunt sociological discourse. One of the most salient among them is the contorted interpretation of the 'rationalization theory' bequeathed to contemporary sociologists by Max Weber, one of those great thinkers who were acutely aware of the sociological (as distinct from psychological, existential or otherwise individual-centred) ambiguity of free choice guided by means–ends calculus. In most commentaries, social contradictions spotted by Weber in the 'rationalizing tendency' are interpreted in the spirit of Romanticism — as free individuals tussling in the tight net of scientifically prescribed and efficiency-bound rules; as another screening of the old 'individual versus society' drama. Once this has been done, it is only too easy to castigate Weber for the equivocality and inconsistency of his analyses. Inconsistency, however, lies in an interpretation alien to the true content of Weber's analysis.

Weber entertained no illusions as to the feasibility of turning free choice and reason-guided, rational action into the universal property of every member of modern society. In the neat and apposite assessment of Whimster and Lash,

Weber candidly admitted that science was an affair of the intellectual aristocracy. Politics was a special calling, and only few individuals were suited to its joint demands of rational responsibility and commitment to freely chosen beliefs. Of the arts Weber was decidedly highbrow.[15]

To Weber, the direct, willing, freely chosen application of reason to one's own action was an option which was and will remain open only to a selected minority. Whimster and Lash point out one of the considerations which informed such judgement: not all people are capable of lifting themselves to the high intellectual level which reason simultaneously makes possible and demands. Only some people have the necessary qualities of mind and character. This was not, however, Weber's only consideration; moreover, it was one which could be declared out of court (for its barely concealed aristocratic or élitist affinities) without undermining the validity of Weber's belief in the selectivity of free and rational individual behaviour. Martin Albrow puts his finger on the truly decisive consideration, when he states that 'the material means for making use of the freedom provided by the rationalised state are distributed in unequal fashion' and warns against 'any attempt to resolve the argument that isolates the formal issue of rationality and freedom from the material facts of the ownership and control of property.'[16]

The crucial point to make about Weber's vision of rationally organized society is that it does *not* allow for making freedom and rational action into the properties of all and any member of the society. Rationality in the social system requires — and allows — freedom and rationality of action of its leaders and designers. As to the rest of its members, their behaviour must be regulated by rationally designed and codified rules which shape the external context of conduct in such a way as to elicit behaviour compatible with the logic of the system. A rational system is a *rationalized* system. It needs the freedom and individual rationality of its rationalizers to secure rational conditions of life (yet not necessarily freedom) for the rest of its members.

Contrary to frequently voiced opinions, there is no inconsistency or contradiction in Weber's scheme between rational freedom of choice on the one hand and the stultifying, suffocating world of bureaucracy on the other (for Weber, an ideal model of bureaucracy was an exercise in spelling out the rules which a rationally organized society should follow — compare the brilliant analysis recently supplied by David Beetham[17]). Freedom can be neither effective nor secure without solidifying mastery gained through the imposition of regulations, regimenting the future behaviour of those over whom the mastery has been gained. Regulations, on the other hand, would be blind and purposeless were they not given meaning by free agents capable of choice-making, and so of giving direction and purpose to the otherwise impassive and directionless, neutrally-technical, machinery. Freedom and bureaucratic regimentation complement each other. In a rational system they may only exist together — the first confined to a receptacle safely perched on the roof of the bureaucratic edifice, and insulated against the danger of leaking which could cause the building to decompose and decay.

The reader will presumably spot the considerable similarity between the two-tiered model of rational society as theorized by Weber, and the vision of rational society depicted by Jeremy Bentham in his parable *Panopticon*. Each model is held together by a strict separation of two distinct yet complementary principles of organization; each accommodates freedom and unfreedom as its equally indispensable constituents; and each does without 'spiritual unity' of the allegiance-to-common-values sort, relying on the assumed self-interestedness of individuals as a sufficient condition of its proper functioning (it has not been emphasized strongly enough that the 'legal-rational legitimation of authority', which Weber postulated for the modern, rational society, sounds a death knell to the traditional image of legitimation as a set of substantive beliefs and policy choices). In each of the two models, selectively allocated individual freedom is seen first and foremost as a functional factor in securing rationality of the system as a whole. Freedom is deployed in the service of designing and enforcing constraints which are trusted to elicit desirable (beneficial, useful, efficient) conduct on every level of the system.

3
Profits and Costs of Freedom

The desire for freedom comes from the experience of oppression, that is from the feeling that one cannot escape doing what one would rather not do (or cannot refrain from doing it without exposing oneself to a penalty which is even more unpleasant than surrender to the original demand), or from the feeling that one cannot do what one would wish to do (or one cannot do it without exposing oneself to a penalty more painful than the abstention from action).

One can sometimes locate the source of oppression in the people one knows – people with whom one comes into a direct communicative contact. Small, intimate groups which one forms or enters willingly – hoping to escape the cumbersome rules and formal patterns of 'public life', and thus to lay down arms, relax, vent one's true feelings – may soon turn into sources of oppression in their own right. In the words of Barrington Moore Jr:

> Among intimate groups and even loving couples common experience shows that friendly warmth can with the passage of time turn into highly charged hostility. Protection can turn into oppression. One reason for this transformation is sheer boredom and satiety. Another . . . is the breakdown of cooperative relationships.[1]

In our own complex, functionally divided society, the need for 'friendly warmth' which only intimate groups or couples can offer is possibly stronger than even before. However, so is the probability of such groups turning into a new and sinister fount of oppression. Groups are overloaded with expectations which are virtually impossible to meet, and which, once frustrated, lead to mutual recrimination. In the previously quoted study Nicklas Luhmann traced such an overburdening of contemporary intimacy to the fact that it is in the loving/loved partner that people now seek the approval and 'social confirmation' of their individual identity.

In other cases the experience of oppression may be diffuse, 'unanchorable', coming from no clear source. One feels hard done by but sees nobody in particular to blame, except for the anonymous 'they' (who merely deputize for the admission of one's ignorance). This notorious difficulty in locating the culprits of many an obvious wrong-doing John Lachs explains by the 'mediation of action' – the fact that in a complex society with multi-dimensional and minutely refined division of labour the initiative for and the actual performance of most actions seldom coincide in one person; as a rule there is a long social distance between the command and its fulfilment, between the design and its implementation, a distance filled by numerous people, each with only a feeble knowledge of the original intention and final destination of the activity to which they contribute (the alternative way of thinking of 'mediated action' would be in terms of 'extended chains of dependence', which according to Norbert Elias characterize our modern society):

> The remarkable thing is that we are not unable to recognize wrong acts or gross injustices when we see them. What amazes us is how they could have come about when each of us did none but harmless acts. We look for someone to blame them, for conspiracies that may explain the horrors we all abhor. It is difficult to accept that often there is no person and no group that planned or caused it all.[2]

Whenever in spite of keen effort we fail to 'personalize' the blame, we tend to speak of *social* oppression; an oppression which follows from the very existence of society, as a sort of unavoidable, natural necessity (when we intend to do nothing about it); or an oppression which results from a flawed organization of society (when we still hope to eliminate it).

However one accounts for the feeling of oppression, the roots of the feeling always lie in the clash between one's own intentions (or intentions experienced as one's own), and the possibility to act on them. Such a clash is what ought to be expected in a society in which practically everybody is 'socially displaced', being continually exposed to uncoordinated and often contradictory demands and pressures coming from semi-autonomous functional sectors of the greater society, and to mutually incompatible evaluations of such demands and pressures. Paradoxically the same society which, thanks to its functional differentiation, leaves to the individual a lot of choice and makes him a truly 'free' individual, also generates on a massive scale the experience of oppression.

When the experience of oppression is common, so is the drive for freedom. The meaning of freedom remains clear as long as it is thought of as the redress of oppression; as removal of this or that specific constraint, at odds with an intention most intensely felt and most painfully frustrated at the moment. It is less easy to visualize freedom positively, as a durable state. All attempts to do so invariably lead to contradictions to which no convincing solution has been found so far.

'Complete freedom' can only be imagined (though not practised) as full solitude: total abstention from communication with other people. Such a state is untenable even in theory. First, liberation from social ties would leave the 'free' person alone against the overwhelming odds of nature; other people, however noxious and obtrusive they may be as a source of unwelcome demands, are also resources without which the effort of purely physical survival would be doomed. Second, it is in communication with other people that the affirmation of one's choices is established and actions are given meanings. However personal one's purposes may seem, they are always borrowed rather than invented, or at least given sense in retrospect by the consent of some social grouping (or they are refused consent, in which case further devotion to the questioned purpose would be socially classified as a case of madness). Persistent separation from human company would therefore involve the twin curses of lack of protection and of growing uncertainty, each one sufficient to turn any imaginable gains of freedom into loss.

If complete freedom is a mental experiment rather than a practical experience, freedom in a more attenuated form is practised under the name of 'privacy'. Privacy is the right to refuse the intrusion of other people (as individuals, or as agents of some supra-individual authority) into specific places, at specific times or during specific activities. While enjoying privacy, the individual may be 'out of sight', certain of not being watched, and thus able to engage in whatever one may wish to engage in, without fear of reprobation. Privacy is as a rule partial – intermittent, confined to special places or selected aspects of life. Beyond certain limits, it may turn into solitude, and thus offer a taste of some of the horrors of imaginary 'complete' freedom. Privacy serves best the function of an antidote to social pressures, when one can move freely in and out of it; when privacy remains truly an interlude between periods of social engagement; preferably, an interlude one can fix in the time of one's choice.

Privacy is costly, and literally so. Some people are forcibly deprived of it, and thus exposed to the relentless vigilance of external controls, like the inmates of Bentham's panopticon; prisons, military barracks, hospitals, mental clinics, schools are all institutions where the prevention of privacy looms large among the techniques deployed in the service of declared ends. The absence of force-backed prohibitions does not mean, however, that privacy is freely available. Privacy requires 'refuges' (Orest Ranum[3]), like private rooms, enclosed gardens, recesses, woods guarded against intruders – spaces marked for personal use only and effectively protected from 'trespassing'. Access to such spaces is always a matter of privilege and luxury; only the rich and the powerful may assume that the alternative of privacy is constantly available as a matter of fact. For the rest, privacy, even if a viable proposition, is problematic – a distant target, the goal of strenuous effort and sacrifice.

Privacy is costly, however, also in the sense of other personal needs which must be traded off in its name. Above all, privacy requires at least temporary suspension of social intercourse; there is no one to share one's dreams, worries or fears with, to offer succour or protection. Privacy is bearable only thanks to the hope that return to the company of others, the opportunity to share one's thoughts and aims with others, is always possible. The subjective costs of that oppression which is the price attached to all communication, tend to diminish as the length of privacy grows.

The general picture emerging out of the above consideration is one of ambivalence. Abhorrence of oppression is balanced by the dread of loneliness; disaffection with imposed conformity tends to be cancelled out by the anxiety brought by responsibility one cannot share with others. Looking at the inherent ambiguity of freedom from the other side, George Balandier pointed to its kinship with an equally persistent ambivalence of all, however oppressive, power. Power offers, so to speak, 'freedom from freedom': it brings release from the responsibility for choice – which is always harrowing and often too risky for one's liking. Precisely *because* it can be oppressive, and hence efficient in its oppressiveness, power may be viewed as a guarantee of regularity, experienced as order and security; for this it tends to be accepted, even if, at the same time, it is resented and contested as the guardian of a *specific* version of order, in which controversial issues are resolved against one's interests. Acceptance and challenge do not just alternate in one's attitude to power; most of the time they are present together, blending uneasily in one's relations to power as they do in one's attitude toward freedom. 'All political regimes express this ambiguity, whether they conform to tradition or to bureaucratic rationality'.[4]

The two cases of ambivalence, one associated with the experience of freedom and the other with the constraints linked to all group membership, continually generate the dream of community; a special kind of community, as it were, which bears no resemblance to any real communities known to historians or anthropologists (in Mary Douglas's curt verdict, 'small-scale societies do not exemplify the idealised vision of community'[5]). The fantasy, bred and fed by the disconcerting ambiguity of freedom, conjures up a community which puts paid to fear of loneliness *and* horror of oppression at the same time; a community which does not simply 'balance out' the two unpalatable extremes but effectively writes them off for good; a community in which freedom *and* togetherness can be enjoyed simultaneously – both coming, so to speak, free of charge. Dreamt-of communities of this kind serve as illusory solutions to a contradiction always encountered and never conclusively resolved in the reality of daily life. Such dreams are often falsely interpreted as manifestations of nostalgia, and then dismissed on the ground of historical inaccuracy. In fact, their roots stick firmly in present realities, which is why illusory communities help us to understand better quite real contradictions embedded in modern social life.

The need for freedom and the need for social interaction – inseparable, though often at odds with each other – seem to be a permanent feature of the human condition. Roughly speaking, the poignancy with which each of them is felt depends on the degree to which the other is fulfilled or exceeded. The balance between them changes as we move from one historical era to another, or from one society to another. The capitalist revolution inflamed the popular imagination with the vision of freedom from the iniquities of rank and the wearisome meddling of corporations or parishes. With such constraints broken and discarded, most people found, however, that freedom meant the necessity to rely on one's own resources, which was all right as far as one had resources to rely on. For many, strong power once more became a priority – and a would-be dictator

who promised the perplexed a solid dose of law, order and
certainty, stood a good chance of being widely heard and avidly
listened to.

Which way does the pendulum tend to move in the kind of society
we live in? Is it freedom or communal togetherness which we miss
more? Has our society, with its freedom to pursue wealth and social
importance, with its free competition and ever-growing range of
consumer choice, supplied all the freedom one may desire? Is the
satisfaction of the other need, that of communal support, the last
task still left on the social agenda?

A clear-cut answer to this question is not easy to find and more
difficult still to substantiate. Subtle shifts in cognitive perspective
(between aspects of life, or the categories of people whose situation
is focused on) may lead to widely divergent views. Many observers
point out with good reason that capitalism, particularly in its
consumer phase, opened up for most people the possibility to
exercise their wit, will and judgement to an extent never heard of
before (compare, for instance, Bryan S. Turner's comments on the
role of consumer choice in the enhancement of individual
freedom[6]). Others emphasize, with equally good reason, the
tremendous strides in social control over individual life which have
been made possible by the spectacular advances of information
technology, the so-called 'caring professions' and, indeed, a new
version of 'social Taylorism', aimed this time at consumer
behaviour. The following quotation from Robins and Webster's
study is an unusually well-balanced and moderate expression of that
view:

> spheres of life have become more consciously and systematically
> regulated, more distinctly managed than in the past (when hunger,
> oppression and the tyranny of nature were major means of control),
> the better to predict, guide, act upon, and take advantage of people's
> desires, wants, motives and actions. Our view is that control is more
> integrated into social relations than previously and that, though this
> may not take a harsh or even an unpleasant form, it is more extensive
> than before, such that even 'escape attempts' from the routine and
> predictable arena of work into hobbies, holidays, fantasies etc. are
> usually packaged and scripted.[7]

A somewhat separate current in recent analyses concerns itself
not so much with the global amount of freedom or unfreedom
contemporary society produces, as with the changing character of
such freedoms as this society may provide. The reader may

remember from the preceding chapter that the modern version of freedom was marked by a close association with individuality and capitalism; yet it is precisely this link which is proclaimed now as fast disappearing. Whatever freedom we can find in our society — so it is said — it is certainly not taking the form of the self-assertive, independent, sovereign individual which we considered its most conspicuous embodiment since the dawn of modern times and capitalist society. And so Abercrombie, Hill and Turner suggest that 'Individualism and capitalism no longer serve each other. Capitalism has outgrown individualism and is now less shaped by it than it was before. Indeed, there are signs that individualism in the modern world may be dysfunctional for capitalism'. They conclude, 'there is a progressive erosion of the area of liberty and a corresponding retreat into what private world is left'.[8]

Without spelling out a similar hypothesis, Norbert Elias has advanced a theory which depicts a progressive divorce between capitalism and the 'sovereign individual' as inevitable. Indeed, the survival of the latter is impossible, if the principle which defines the first ('free competition') is applied without qualification. This is a powerful theory, grounded in a perceptive analysis of profuse historical evidence, and developed with impeccable logic.

Pivotal concepts of Elias's theory are 'elimination contest' and 'monopoly function'. Though it had been developed mainly to account for the passage from feudal dispersion to the absolutist state, it was located at a high level of generality: the final outcome was explained in terms of the inner logic of a figuration which consists of a number of independent units engaged in unconstrained competition with each other:

> a society with numerous power and property units of relatively equal size, tends under strong competitive pressures towards an enlargement of a few units and finally towards monopoly. . . . A human figuration in which a relatively large number of units, by virtue of the power at their disposal, are in competition, tends to deviate from this state of equilibrium (many balanced by many; relatively free competition) and to approach a different state in which fewer and fewer units are able to compete. . . .
>
> The human figuration caught up in this movement will . . . unless countervailing measures are taken, approach a state in which all opportunities are controlled. . . . A system with open opportunities has become a system with closed opportunities . . . .

> [A]n ever increasing number of power chances tend to accumulate
> in the hands of an ever-diminishing number of people through a
> series of elimination contests.[9]

Those many who lost the contest now become servants of the few
who won. Which means that even if the figuration starts from a state
of perfect equality between its constituent units (which is never a
case in practice), it will inevitably end up as a set of few powerful
units and a lot of dispossessed ones, now transformed into
subordinates whose action is regimented and certainly not
'sovereign' any more. On a smaller scale, we have seen recently a
striking example of Elias's 'elimination contest' principle in action.
'Deregulation', executed in the name of increased competition, led
quickly and invariably to the formation of a few gigantic con-
glomerates which between themselves monopolized the lion's share
of the field and to all practical intents and purposes put an end to the
idea of 'independent entrepreneurs' (as in the case of the American
airlines or London stockbrokers).

With the 'elimination contest' and 'monopoly function' in
operation, one would expect the typically capitalist rendering of
individual freedom to be confined to a progressively smaller part of
the population. The times of the lonely tycoons, pulling themselves
up to the highest reaches of society by their bootstraps, are over.
Self-made tycoons are dead even as a myth, as heroes of popular
dreams. Students of contemporary literature aimed at a mass
readership note the virtually complete disappearance of interest in
the old-style success story of the 'pioneers of industry' kind;
together with such interest disappears the once widely held belief in
the personal qualities of individual character as decisive factors of
successful life. In the words of John G. Cavelti:

> No popular ideal had yet emerged to take the place once held by the
> philosophy of success. Instead, it seemed that the ideal of the
> self-made man had gradually eroded without generating a new
> standard for the determination of individual and social goals. . . .
> Today's office boy knows that a year at Harvard Business School will
> do more for his career than a lifetime of industry, economy,
> temperance, and piety.[10]

For most people who, were they alive a century and a half ago,
would probably have engaged in the ruthless competitive struggle
for wealth and power, the road to an agreeable life now leads
through excelling in conformity to institutionally set purposes, rules

and patterns of conduct. In order to succeed, they have to surrender what the self-made hero of entrepreneurial capitalism considered an inalienable part of freedom. They also have to put up with a much greater dose of oppression than their entrepreneurial ancestors would have been prepared to live with. They have to accept commands, demonstrate a willingness to obey, cut their own actions to the measure designed by their superiors. However high they rise in riches, power or fame, they remain conscious that they are 'being seen', observed and censored, like the middle-rank supervisors in Bentham's panopticon. The traditional capitalist pattern of freedom is not for them. Their own drive to freedom must seek other outlets, find new forms. There are few, if any, virgin plots left in the land where wealth is made. It does not necessarily mean, however, that no alternative room for freedom has been provided.

The individual's drive to self-assertion has been squeezed out from the area of material production. Instead, a wider than ever space has been opened for it at the new 'pioneer frontier', the rapidly expanding, seemingly limitless, world of consumption. In this world capitalism seems to find, at last, the secret of the philosophers' stone: seen from the vantage-point of the consumers, the consumer world (unlike the area of production and distribution of wealth and power) is free from the curse of elimination contest and monopoly function. Here, contest may go on and on without elimination; and the number of its participants may indeed grow instead of shrinking. As if this was not a sufficiently formidable achievement, the world of consumption seems to have cured freedom from another affliction: insecurity. In its consumer version, individual freedom may be exercised without sacrificing that certainty which lies at the bottom of spiritual security. These two truly revolutionary achievements lend legitimation to the opinion that late capitalist society in its consumerist phase offers a space for human freedom larger than any other known society, past or present.

The remarkable freedom of the consumer world from the self-annihilating tendency of all other forms of competition has been achieved through lifting inter-individual rivalry from wealth and power (goods which are by nature in limited supply, and hence liable to the unstoppable monopolization drive) to symbols. In the world of consumption, the possession of goods is only one of the stakes of the competition. The fight is also about symbols, about differences and distinctions they signify. As such, this competition has a unique capacity for propagating its own stakes rather than gradually using them up in the course of the fight.

Many years before consumerism finally came into its own, one of the most perceptive American sociologists, Thornstein Veblen, spotted this potential for symbolic competition: 'since the struggle is substantially a race for respectability on the basis of invidious comparison, no approach to a definitive attainment is possible'.[11] Never conclusive, always supplied with fresh stimulations and forever keeping hopes alive, the struggle may be eternally self-perpetuating, drawing its purpose and energy from its own momentum. This mechanism of self-propulsion and self-perpetuation has been subjected to minute and penetrating scrutiny by a leading French sociologist, Pierre Bourdieu.[12] The gist of his conclusion is that the differences between social positions, rather than the positions themselves, are the true stakes of the competition as defined by the world of consumption; and 'Differences of situation and above all of position, are on a symbolic level the object of a systematic expansion'.[13] There is no end to the number of positional differences. In principle, no scarce natural resources or constraints of available wealth need limit it. Ever new differences are produced in the course of the rivalry between consumers, and hence the prizes gained by some rivals do not necessarily diminish the chances of the others. On the contrary, they stimulate the rest to ever stronger and more determined efforts. Partaking of rivalry, rather than the material trophies which symbolize the momentary state of the game, is what makes the distinction.

Marc Guillaume suggested that in the phase of consumerism the 'utility function' of goods purchased on the market is eclipsed, while the 'sign function' is taking pride of place.[14] It is the signs which are coveted, sought after, purchased and consumed. We can say that the goods are desired not for their capacity to enhance one's body or mind (make them healthier, richer, more fulsome), but for their magic potential to give a particular, distinguished and hence desired, shape to the body or the spirit (a particular look which serves as a badge of belonging on the right side of the difference). We can also go beyond Guillaume and propose that the very distinction between the 'utility' and the 'sign' functions does not make much sense in view of the fact that it is precisely the signifying capacity which constitutes the main attraction, indeed the true 'utility function' of marketable goods.

Shifting the area of individual freedom from competition for wealth and power to symbolic rivalry creates an entirely new possibility for individual self-assertion; one which never faces the danger of imminent and conclusive defeat and hence does not necessarily carry the seed of frustration and self-destruction. Theorizing consumer rivalry as 'not really a true freedom', as a compensation for stifling the 'real competition', as a product of deception or a conspiracy of big merchandising companies, will change little, whatever its truth. The rivalry, the individual energy it summons, the variety of choices it makes possible, the personal gratification it brings, are all real enough. They are enjoyed, cherished, seen as tantamount to self-assertion and would not be easily surrendered — certainly not in exchange for a regimentation of needs and a rationing of satisfactions.

We can now somewhat modify our previous, preliminary consideration of the historical fate of the original marriage between capitalism and the freedom of the individual. The marriage did not end in a divorce. It is, on the contrary, alive and well. What did happen instead is something only to be expected in long marriages: both partners went through a series of transformations which, for someone who met them again now for the first time since their marriage, would seem to have changed them beyond recognition. Capitalism is not defined today by competition. It has been a long time since it stopped to be a 'free for all', a frontier with no limit in sight, a fertile soil for ingenuity, initiative and sheer muscle power. It is instead a highly organized system, steered and monitored from a limited (and still shrinking) number of control centres, each armed with ever more potent and costly technological means of gathering and producing information. Capitalist competition seems to have come close to the purpose of all competition: to work itself, so to speak, out of a job; to end with itself. This aim has been approximated at least to the point at which the entry of new competitors becomes exceedingly difficult — so that competition in its traditional, early-capitalist form, becomes a proposition unfit for mass distribution.

But the other partner of the marriage has changed as well. The self-assertive individual of the early capitalist era, concerned with establishing his own identity and getting it socially approved, is still very much alive — he only seeks the resolution of his problems in another sphere of life, and accordingly employs different tools. If anything, freedom of choice, and the self-assertive way of life which goes with it, is today an option open and accessible to a much larger section of society than in the times of the pioneers. However hard the 'rags to riches' preachers tried to convince us to the contrary, the number of people who could truly exercise their freedom in capitalist competition was always extremely limited. The time of pioneers and tycoons was also a time when the overwhelming majority of society's members were confined for the duration of their lives to the bottom echelons of the panopticon-like hierarchy. Freedom was a privilege and except for a few unique and always short-lived cases (like 'western frontier' of the United States), a privilege accessible to very few. One cannot even be sure whether the total number of those who availed themselves of the privilege showed any downward tendency over the years, as is often implied. It may be that the number remained fairly constant and is still as large (or, rather, as small) as at any time in the past. What is mistaken for the demise of the bold, tough and pushing self-made entrepreneur, is a twofold change in the ideology, rather than practice, of capitalist society. First, stubborn evidence has been in the end admitted, and the self-consciousness of capitalist society has reconciled itself to the fact that the unique life-stories of a few spectacularly successful tycoons will never turn into a universal pattern of personal success for the masses. Second, the old 'entrepreneurial' pattern of success lost a good deal of popularity together with its exclusiveness. Other, equally attractive and more realistic patterns appeared, better fit for mass distribution.

Among these other patterns, one stands out as in many respects superior to the old: the pattern of success as symbolic distinction, attainable through consumer rivalry — a success attainable (to use Max Weber's terms) not through internal class competition and interclass struggle but through rivalry inside, and taste-contest between, status groups. The superiority of this pattern of success over the one traditionally associated with capitalism, and actively promoted in the first half of its history, is striking. The new pattern does not simply replace the old as an efficient guide of individual behaviour; it is the first pattern of individual freedom and self-assertion which can be followed, not just in ideologically induced fantasies but in practical life, by the *majority* in capitalist society. Far from suppressing the potential for individual expansion, capitalism brought about a kind of society in which the life-pattern of free choice and self-assertion can be practised on a scale unheard of before. This, however, is a development closely linked to the substitution of symbolic rivalry for the competition for wealth and power; to the setting aside, in other words, of a special reserve where free individuals may operate unconstrained, and without damaging the basic network of power relations where the principles of elimination contest and monopoly function remain reliable guarantees of stability.

From this rearrangement, capitalism emerges strengthened. Excessive strain generated by the power contest has been channelled away from the central power structures and onto a safe ground, where tensions can be unloaded without adversely affecting the administration of power resources. The deployment of energy released by free individuals engaged in symbolic rivalry lifts demand for the products of capitalist industry to ever higher levels, and effectively emancipates consumption from all 'natural' limits defined by the capacity of 'material needs' — those needs which require goods solely as 'utility values'. Last though not least, with consumption firmly established as a focus and the playground for individual freedom, the future of capitalism looks more secure than ever. Social control becomes an easier task. Costly, 'panoptical' methods of control, pregnant as they are with dissent, may be disposed of, or replaced by a less costly and more efficient method of seduction (or, rather, the deployment of 'panoptical' methods may be limited to a minority of the population, which for whatever reason cannot be integrated through the consumer market). The soliciting of conduct functionally indispensable for the capitalist economic system and harmless to the capitalist political system may now be entrusted to the consumer market and its attractions. Reproduction of the capitalist system is therefore achieved through individual freedom and not through its suppression. Instead of being recorded on the side of systemic overheads, the whole operation of 'social control' may be now counted among systemic assets.

What makes the consumer market a form of control which those who are to be controlled by it willingly and enthusiastically embrace, is not just the shine and the beauty of the rewards it offers for obedience. Its main attraction, perhaps, is that it offers freedom to people who in other areas of their life find only constraints, often experienced as oppression. What makes the freedom offered by the market more alluring still is that it comes without the blemish which tainted most of its other forms: the same market which offers freedom offers also certainty. It offers the individual the right to a 'thoroughly individual' choice; yet it also supplies social approval for such choice, thereby exorcizing that ghost of insecurity which (as we saw at the beginning of this chapter) poisons the joy of the sovereign will. In a paradoxical way, the consumer market meets the bill of that 'fantasy community' where freedom and certainty, independence and togetherness live alongside each other without conflict. People are thus pulled to the market by a double bind: they depend on it for their individual freedom; and they depend on it for enjoying their freedom without paying the price of insecurity.

We remember that having shattered the communal or corporative fetters fastening people to their ascribed position well-nigh permanently, modern times faced the individuals with the harrowing task of constructing their own social identity. Everyone has to answer for himself the question 'who am I', 'how should I live', 'who do I want to become' — and, at the end of the day, be prepared to accept responsibility for the answer. In this sense, freedom is for the modern individual the fate he cannot escape, except by retreating into a fantasy world or through mental disorders. Freedom is, therefore, a mixed blessing. One needs it to be oneself; yet being oneself solely on the strength of one's free choice means a life full of doubts and fears of error.

There are many ways in which one can respond to the task of constructing self-identity. To be adequate to the task, however, selected ways must include some criteria by which the success of the whole enterprise can be appraised, and the outcome of self-construction approved. Self-construction of the self is, so to speak, a necessity. Self-confirmation of the self is an impossibility.

Few of the theoretically possible responses to the task of self-construction meet that additional condition. One which most certainly does is the self-assertive response: an effort to force one's own project, one's own conception of the world, upon other people, thereby subjecting them to one's own will — instead of finding one's way through reality, to remould reality to one's own measure, 'leaving one's imprint on the world'. This was, allegedly, the way of capitalist pioneers, romantic artists and political demagogues. The obvious weakness of such a response (whatever its true or imaginary virtues) is that it may be chosen only by a few; indeed, it makes sense only on condition that the majority of people constitute the selfsame reality which is to be shaped, remoulded, subjected to rule, 'imprinted upon'. It is their passivity and obedience which serves as the confirmation of the few heroic selves; their conformity is the sought-after proof of someone else's self-assertion. Decidedly, the self-assertive response cannot be thought of as a universal way of dealing with the task of self-construction.

The method of tackling the task of self-construction offered by the consumer market is free from such limitations; it can be, in principle, employed by everybody, and by all at the same time. The market method consists in selecting symbols of identity from the large pool of goods on offer. Selected symbols can be put together in all sorts of ways, thus making possible a great number of 'unique combinations'. For virtually every projected self, there are purchasable signs to express it. If, for the time being, they are missing, one can rely on the profit-guided logic of the market to supply them shortly.

The market way consists, as it were, in building up the self using images. The self becomes identical with visual clues other people can see and recognize as meaning whatever they are intended to mean. Visual clues are of many kinds. They include the shape of one's body, bodily adornments, the type and contents of one's home, the places one attends and where one can be seen, the way one behaves or talks, what one talks about, one's demonstrable artistic and literary taste, the food one eats and the fashion in which the food is prepared — and many other things, all supplied by the market in the form of material goods, services or knowledge. Moreover, single clues come complete with instructions on how to assemble them into total images. No individual ought to feel handicapped by the poverty of his imagination — model identities are also supplied by the market, and the only job left to be done by the individual himself is to follow the instruction attached to the kit. The freedom to choose one's identity therefore becomes a realistic proposition. There is a range of options to choose from, and once the choice has been made, the selected identity can be made real (i.e. symbolically real, real as perceptible image) by making the necessary purchases or subjecting oneself to the required drills — be it a new hair-style, jogging routine, slimming diet or enriching one's speech with currently fashionable status-symbolizing vocabulary.

This freedom differs from previously discussed forms in that it does not lead to a 'zero-sum' game, that is to a game in which one can gain only as much as someone else must lose. In the game of consumer freedom all customers may be winners at the same time. Identities are not scarce goods. If anything, their supply tends to be excessive, as the overabundance of any image is bound to detract from its value as a symbol of individual uniqueness. Devaluation of an image is never a disaster, however, as discarded images are immediately followed by new ones, as yet not too common, so that self-construction may start again, hopeful as ever to attain its purpose: the creation of a unique selfhood. Hence the universality of the market solution to the problem of individual freedom — and the apparent absence of the self-destructive tendencies we have detected in other solutions.

Social approval of free choices (i.e. freedom from uncertainty), is another service the market offers to its consumers. This service is free. Approval comes together with the identity kits, like assembling briefs.

The symbols are associated in the cognitive maps of prospective customers with the types of life the customers wish to achieve with their help. Elements of the final image are carefully pre-assembled before they are put on display; they are shown 'in a context', alongside easily recognizable signs of the situations which they promise to provide, so that the link gradually sediments in the customers' mind (or subconscious) as 'natural', 'evident', calling for no further argument or justification. The situation in question seems from now on incomplete without a given commodity (a successful party without a particular brand of wine; family bliss without a particular brand of washing powder; caring father and husband without a particular insurance policy; beautiful, youthful skin without a particular fragrance, etc.). More importantly still, the commodities in question seem from now on to blend with the situation itself; on top of their own attractions, they offer confidence that the situation of which they are an organic part will indeed be achieved.

The value of some other commodity-symbols is asserted on the authority of well-known public personalities, already enjoying public esteem to the point of becoming patterns for popular emulation; or on the authority of science, to which the possession of reliable and unquestionable knowledge is attributed. The advertisement for the product is introduced by a famous person who assures the audience that he/she is using it regularly and successfully, or even that the personal success for which this person is famous has been achieved thanks to the use of the product (a great athlete gaining his strength from drinking a particular nourishing concoction; a popular actress maintaining her beauty thanks to a certain face cream). Alternatively, the advertisement invokes an unspecified 'scientific survey', refers obliquely to the opinion of 'the doctors', 'the dentists' or, even more generally, to images of modern (or futuristic) technology, already established in the public mind as the epitome of solid, trustworthy knowledge (sometimes, it is enough to use an ostensibly 'scientific' jargon to create the visibility of rational reasoning — like 'this detergent will wash whiter because it contains a special ingredient which washes whiter',[15] or for more sophisticated customers, to print a description of an expensive car in a foreign language and sprinkle it generously with what seem to be physical equations or algebraic formulae). The outcome is not just the customer's certainty that the product well serves its declared purpose; there is also a net gain for the psychological well-being of the customer: a product obtainable in the shops becomes a true embodiment of rationality, and its use as a symbol of rational behaviour. Whoever uses the product, partakes of the prestige of the foremost authority of our times. One can become rational simply by the act of right purchase; one can buy certainty together with the product. Free choice becomes a well-informed choice without sacrificing the freedom of the chooser, in the same way as freedom does not need to endanger anymore one's self-assurance — the conviction that the choices are right and rational.

A similar effect of subjective certainty may be achieved by evoking the authority of numbers. In this case the prestige of the democratic vote is harnessed in the service of consumer certainty. Commercials inform the prospective customer that so many per cent of the population (always a majority) use a given product; or that 'more and more' people 'switch' to the product. Great numbers carry authority simply by their size; the shared (though seldom spelt out) assumption is that 'so many people cannot be wrong', particularly if they are in a majority. The paramount function of the argument-through-numbers is not however to imbue certainty of the kind induced with the help of scientific authority. Percentages and majorities are quoted as symbols of social approval; they deputize for the once so powerful, now weakened or missing, communal support negotiated in the past through face-to-face interaction. Tightly structured communities have been atomized and transformed into 'populations' — loose aggregates of unconnected individuals. At this stage their authority can be only construed by counting percentages, and can only speak through the results of opinion polls. It claims nevertheless, and with a measure of success, the prestige once lodged in communal verdicts. The borrowed prestige of community allows the quantitative argument to serve as a reliable foundation for individual certainty.

The consumer market is therefore a place where freedom and certainty are offered and obtained together; freedom comes free of pain, while certainty can be enjoyed without detracting from the conviction of subjective autonomy. This is no mean achievement of the consumer market; no other institution has gone this far towards the resolution of the most malignant of the many antinomies of freedom.

It goes without saying that the market does not provide its unique service for the love of its consumers (though many companies follow the example of 'smiling banks' and 'banks who like to say yes' in trying to convince the clients that this is exactly what motivates their conduct). Neither is the wedding of freedom and certainty — so crucial for the role played by the consumer market in controlling and integrating late capitalist society — the result of a political ploy or carefully designed propaganda campaign. The consumer market offers its unique service to the political stability of capitalism and the social integration of its members 'on the way' to its own profit-subordinated aims. The service is, so to speak, a 'side-effect', a 'by-product' of the rationally organized pursuit of growing demand and increased revenue. The certainty the market supplies is not offered unconditionally; invariably, it is structured in such a way as to include, as its indispensable ingredient, the purchase of a certain product. The act of purchase is presented as the *only* road to certainty. Those who refrain from purchase *cannot* be sure of behaving reasonably; more than that, they ought to understand that they are *not* rational beings, that they misuse their freedom and undertake enormous risk which will cost them dearly. In Michael Parenti's vivid description:

> The reader of advertising copy and the viewer of commercials discover that they are not doing right for baby's needs or hubby's or wifey's desires; that they are failing in their careers because of poor appearance, sloppy dress, or bad breath; that they are not treating their complexion, hair, or nails properly; that they suffer unnecessary cold misery and headache pains; that they do not know how to make the tastiest coffee, pie, pudding, or chicken dinner; nor, if left to their own devices, would they be able to clean their floors, sinks, and toilets correctly or tend to their lawns, gardens, appliances, and

automobiles. In order to live well and live properly, consumers need corporate producers to guide them. Consumers are taught personal incompetence and dependence on mass-market producers.[16]

Assisted by the impeccably knowledgeable experts it employs, the market offers the passage from ignorance to rationality, from incompetence to the confidence that the individual's projects and desires will be fulfilled. The only thing required to take advantage of this offer is to trust the advice and to follow it obediently.

Each time the offer is taken advantage of, the dependence of the individual on the market and on experts and their knowledge is reproduced and reinforced. Individuals depend on the market and the experts for being individuals – that is, being able to make free choices and make them without undue risk and pyschological costs. Individual freedom becomes an important link in the process of reproduction of the power structure. If single advertisements or commercials promote concrete brands of single products, the overall and long-term impact of market-mediated freedom and certainty is the security of the social system and the stability of its structure of domination. Under the circumstances, the 'panoptical' method of behavioural control (consisting first and foremost in depriving individuals of their freedom of choice) may be suspended.

Not completely, however. The 'seductive' method of control — through the market and the free consumer — requires a certain level of affluence of its objects. Whatever its subjective and systemic advantages, it cannot be extended indiscriminately to all members of society. There is always a level below which the monetary resources of an individual are too small to render freedom of choice truly 'seductive' and hence the control exercised through it, truly effective. A society integrated through the mechanism of consumer seduction is therefore burdened with a margin of people whose behaviour must be controlled through other means, presumably through some version of 'panoptical' technique.

Social welfare is one such version. According to Douglas E. Ashfield's timely reminder, 'one of the major misconceptions about the political development of welfare states cultivated by a short historical perspective is that the rise of social policy to prominence was a socialist accomplishment'.[17] The development of social welfare was vigorously promoted and feebly resisted thanks to its role in reinforcing the power structure, in securing peace and order inside a social system marked by perpetual inequality of social positions and chances. On the one hand, social welfare was the way of paying 'collectively' the social costs of private pursuit of gain (i.e. mitigating the damage suffered by the losers); on the other, social welfare was from the start a method of keeping in check all those who, being 'masterless men' — neither masters nor master's servants — could not be trusted to guide their own actions or to have their actions already guided in the right direction. These people were to be deprived of freedom to choose and put under conditions where their behaviour could be fully determined and constantly under scrutiny.

Nassau Senior wrote in 1841:

> It is to require the man who demands to be supported by the industry and frugality of others to enter an abode provided for him by the public, where all the necessaries of life are amply provided, but excitement and mere amusement are excluded — an abode where he is better lodged, better clothed, and more healthily fed than he would be in his own cottage, but is deprived of beer, tobacco, and spirits and is forced to submit to habits of order and cleanliness — is separated from his usual associates and his usual pastimes, and is subject to labour, monotonous and uninteresting. [18]

These words come from a statement against outdoor relief and in favour of poorhouses — yet the purpose of all relief, tacitly assumed in the above quotation, continued to influence the logic of social welfare long after the episode of poorhouses was over. The purpose was to *force* upon the poor the selfsame habits of orderly conduct which in the case of those somewhat better off would develop as if 'by themselves'. The method proposed for the purpose was to reduce the condition of the poor to the level where the only choice *they* could make was one between remaining alive or not. An additional bonus of such reduction would be to make individual self-reliance that much more attractive by presenting destitution and total dependence as its sole alternative. The world of symbolic consumption needs the support of the symbolic repression of the people on welfare.

The humanistic intentions of many an earnest advocate of social welfare notwithstanding, this purpose, this method and this hope for an extra benefit for systemic integration as a whole, remained with welfare institutions throughout their history. In Britain (the country which proudly identified itself at that time as a 'welfare state' and which gave the world some of the most humane documents of all times, like the famous Beveridge Report), Brian Abel-Smith noted in 1964 that 'While the private sector is wooing the public with trading stamps, muzak and a battery of packaging devices, in the public sector there is still too often an atmosphere of wartime austerity'.[19] Since these words were written, the gap has never stopped growing. The allurements of the private market turned ever more glittering, while the welfare offices became ever more drab, shoddy and repulsive. The unspoken function of welfare — of creating a *difference* and thereby underlining and reinforcing 'the normal', the legitimate, the socially approved — came to the fore and grew in prominence. Whatever doubts one may entertain about the merits of consumer freedom as the formula for sensible life are easily dispelled with one look at the welfare alternative. The less appetizing the second, the sweeter the taste of the first.

An important tendency in the recent history of welfare is the progressive 'infantilization' of its objects. Their expenditures, furnishings, clothes, food, style of life are carefully controlled; their privacy is violated at will by unannounced visits of the experts in health, hygiene, education; welfare payments are offered only in exchange for full confessions and total exposure of the most intimate aspects of life to the inquisitive officials; after all that, payments are set at a level which leaves no room for the recipients' discretion and choice, allowing only for bare necessities. The rules which regulate the welfare process are based on the assumption that the client of welfare is a failed citizen, someone who evidently cannot exercise his own freedom, someone imprudent and improvident, someone who cannot be trusted to be in control of his own actions. Set in operation, such rules accomplish what they assume: they systematically deprive welfare clients of initiative, de-train them in the art of free choice, force them to remain passive and socially useless. Welfare clients can then be presented to the public as a menace and a liability, as 'parasites' feeding on the healthy body of those who contribute to social wealth. As Jean Seaton recently observed, the press campaign against 'scroungers' 'created an apparent unity between taxpayers and workers as it implied they were being exploited by feckless claimants'.[20]

The radical unfreedom of welfare recipients is but an extreme demonstration of a more general regulatory principle which underlies the vitality of the consumer-led social system. Goods and services which are not mediated by the free market (so-called 'public services', or goods aimed for 'collective consumption', like public health, public education, sanitation, public transport, etc., which are unlikely to be sold at a profit, or by their very nature are unfit for selling to individual consumers) tend to fall in quality and lose in attractiveness in both relative and absolute terms. Unlike the goods and services merchandised by the market, they tend to discourage their prospective consumers; to their utility values *negative* symbolic values are attached (stigma falling upon those who are obliged to consume them), so that they appear as a liability in the symbolic rivalry serviced by consumption. The overall shoddiness of public goods and their low grading in the hierarchy of positional symbols tend to encourage everybody who can afford it to 'buy themselves out' of the dependence on public services, and into the consumer market (private car instead of public buses, private health insurance, private education, etc.).

In spite of its universalistic applicability in principle, the freedom of the consumer remains in practice a privilege and a distinction. In a consumer society this is perhaps not a *logical* necessity, but it seems to be a *practical* inevitability. In order to employ consumer freedom as its major medium of social control and integration, the late capitalist system evidently needs to juxtapose freedom with its opposite, oppression; not only to deal with the inescapable side-costs of symbolic rivalry between consumers, but also, and above all, for the symbolic value of the difference. As we saw before, consumer freedom is not an unmixed blessing (this will become more evident still in the next chapter). What makes it a universally preferred choice, and hence a highly effective medium of social control, is precisely its quality as a privilege, a distinction, an escape from a loathsome and repugnant alternative.

Freedom, Society and Social System

In the society we live in, individual freedom moves steadily into the position of the cognitive and moral focus of life — with far-reaching consequences for each individual and for the social system as a whole.

This central place was occupied in the past — during the first part of capitalist history — by work, understood as shared and coordinated effort aimed at the production of wealth through the application of human labour to the remaking of nature.

Work was central to the life of the individual. It made the difference between affluence and indigence, autonomy and dependence, high or low social status, presence or absence of self-esteem. As the only accepted way in which the individual could influence the quality of his life, work was the principal moral norm guiding individual conduct, and the principal vantage-point from which the individual looked at, planned and modelled his life-process as a whole. Thus the worthiness and dignity of one's life was assessed by such criteria as related to work and various aspects of a positive attitude to work: industry, diligence, application, enterprise. Moral disrepute was attached, on the other hand, to refraining from work — denigrated and reviled as idleness, loafing, indolence or sloth. Where individual life was planned, it was life-long vocation which provided the frame. People defined themselves in terms of their occupational skills, the kind of work they acquired the ability to perform. People who shared the same skills and exercised them in the same environment served as the 'significant others'; it was their opinion which counted and was given the authority to evaluate, and if necessary to correct, an individual's life.

On the social plane, the work place provided the major setting for the training and 'socializing' of the individual as a social person. It was there that the virtues of obedience and respect for authority, the habits of self-discipline and the standards of acceptable behaviour were instilled; it was through the work-place that the most meticulous social surveillance and monitoring of individual behaviour took place. Control through the work-place was exercised virtually continuously, as most people spent there a considerable part of their day and most years of their life there. The work-place served, in other words, as the main training-ground for attitudes and actions suitable for the hierarchically differentiated norms of the capitalist society. With work occupying most of the individual's lifetime, and influencing so heavily (both cognitively and morally) the rest of his or her life occupations, the disciplining impact of the work-place could be, by and large, relied upon as a sufficient guarantee of social integration.

Still on the social plane, the work-place served as the natural focal point for the crystallization of social dissent, and the battleground where conflicts could be played out. As the work-place occupied a central position in the individual's life, so did its conflicts; and conflicts could not but be constantly generated by a work-place which functioned as an instrument of bodily and spiritual drill and the suppression of individual autonomy. At the early stage of capitalism, the principal bone of contention was the oppression itself; people subjected to the drill of the capitalist factory wished to retain, or restore, the right to self-determination — a condition still fresh in the memory of yesterday's craftsmen and artisans. Very soon, however, the focus of the conflict was shifted away from the issue of power and control towards that of the distribution of surplus value. The chance of returning to more symmetrical power relations, of undermining the manager's right to rule, dimmed; the acceptance of such a right and reconciliation to a permanently subordinated position inside the factory hierarchy were bought in exchange for a greater share in surplus product. What was initially (and remained in its substance, though not in its ostensible targets) a power conflict became progressively 'economized'.[1] Battles were now carried in the name of better wages, shorter hours, more care for the quality of working conditions. Social integration was attained through compliance, not consent. The power of capital could remain resented as long as it was not contested. The ambitions and hopes of the oppressed were now safely channelled away from the power structure and towards the improvement of

their material standards. This, however, had the largely unanticipated effect of arousing intense consumer interests. Consumer
concerns got a powerful boost from their role as a substitute for
permanently frustrated power ambitions, as the sole recompense
for oppression at work, the only outlet for freedom and autonomy
squeezed out from the largest and the most consequential sector of
the life-process.

The shift from the power contest inside the work-place to
individual rivalry in the world of consumption was a long process; its
direction becomes visible only in retrospect. The history of
capitalism was marked by workers' militancy, best exemplified in
the long struggle of trade unions. Ostensibly, this struggle consist-
ently pursued better wages and better work conditions; ostensibly,
the collectivism of the struggle conducted by trade unions was the
natural response of the workers to the imbalance of power on the
two sides of the great divide, a necessity dictated by the need to
restore the balance of power warped by the employers' monopoly
on work resources. Looked upon from the perspective of their
long-term consequences, however, trade-union struggles seem to
have accomplished something quite different. With every success,
they pushed workers' concerns one more step away from the
power-hierarchy of the work-place toward individual freedom of
choice and autonomy outside the factory; they progressively
'defused' power conflicts, transforming the released energy of
dissent into the pressure aimed at the consumer market. On the
way, trade-union struggle aimed at the salvation, or enhancement,
of the workers' dignity and self-esteem under the conditions of
continuous subordination and refusal of personal autonomy inside
the factory walls. Gradually, however, this theatre of war for
human dignity was conceded to the enemy, the 'managerial
prerogatives' accepted in full. Increasingly, the trade-union effort
focused on securing for its members a privileged existence outside
the work-place[2]: the material conditions necessary to enjoy the
freedom of the consumer, to reassert the autonomy surrendered in
the work-place in the new, magnificent universe of the consumer
market.

On the systemic plane, work was, throughout most of capitalist
history, the central systemic necessity. The maintenance and the
reproduction of economic and political structures depended on
capital engaging the rest of the population in the role of producers.
The surplus product, utilized as the essential resource in the

expansion of the social production of wealth and of support for the social hierarchy of privilege and power, depended on direct subordination of 'living labour' in the process of production. Individuals entered the social system primarily in their role as producers; productive roles were essential units of the system. The power of coercion, monopolized by the political institutions of the state, was deployed above all in the service of 'recommodification' of wealth as *capital* (i.e. such wealth as may be turned to the task of producing more wealth), and of individual members of society as *labour*. The capitalist system constituted its members as actual or potential bearers of producers' roles, relegating all other roles to merely the 'environment' of the productive sphere. Politics deployed socially available resources to service this task; the success or failure of policies, as well as the general 'efficiency' of the state as a whole, could be, and was, measured by the degree to which the task was fulfilled. In effect, the amount of capital invested in production and the number of individuals engaged in the productive process as labour were the main issues of politics and served as the measure of systemic success.

To sum up, throughout the first part of its history, capitalism was characterized by the central position occupied by work simultaneously on the individual, social and systemic planes. Indeed, work served as the link holding together individual motivation, social integration and systemic management, and as the major institution responsible for their mutual congruence and coordination.

It is from this central place that work is being gradually dislodged, as capitalism moves into the consumer phase of its history. Into the vacated room, individual freedom (in its consumer form) has moved. First, perhaps, as a squatter. But more and more as the legitimate resident. In Claus Offe's apt expression, work has been progressively 'decentred'[3] on the individual plane; it has become relatively less important compared to other spheres of life, and confined to a relatively minor position in individual biography; it certainly cannot compete with personal autonomy, self-esteem, family felicity, leisure, the joys of consumption and material possessions as conditions of individual satisfaction and happiness. Work has been, however, 'decentred' also on the social and systemic planes. On every level, consumer freedom moves into its place. It now takes over the crucial role of the link which fastens together the life-worlds of individuals and the purposeful rationality of the system: a major force which coordinates the motivated action of the individual, social integration and the management of the social system.

Of the centrality of consumer freedom in the life of the individual we have already seen quite a lot in the last chapter. Let us recall that the concern with acquisition of the goods and services attainable only through the market has taken the place once occupied by the 'work ethic' (that normative pressure to seek the meaning of life, and the identity of the self, in the role one plays in production, and in the excellence of such role-playing as documented by a successful career). If, in a life normatively motivated by the work ethic, material gains were deemed secondary and instrumental in relation to work itself (their importance consisting primarily in confirming the adequacy of the work effort), it is the other way round in a life guided by the 'consumer ethic'. Here, work is (at best) instrumental; it is in material emoluments that one seeks, and finds, fulfilment, autonomy and freedom. The long-lasting (though perhaps never consummated) marriage between productive work and individual emancipation has ended in divorce. Yet individual emancipation has been wed again; this time, to the consumer market.

Life under the rule of the work ethic was once described by Sigmund Freud as the tragedy of the 'pleasure principle' — truncated, curbed and ultimately suppressed by the 'reality principle'. The innate 'pleasure principle' guided human action towards more sensual satisfaction; it would surely render social life impossible if external constraints were not imposed upon it. Thanks to the threat of coercion, an uneasy and tense compromise is reached between the pleasure principle and the harsh reality of social rules. That oppression which accompanied work for a considerable part of capitalist history Freud generalized as an inevitable feature of all civilization, a necessity rooted in the intrinsic pleasure-orientation of human drives. The masses, wrote Freud, are

> lazy and unintelligent. . . . To put it briefly, there are two wide-spread human characteristics which are responsible for the fact that the regulations of civilisation can only be maintained by a certain degree of coercion — namely, that men are not spontaneously fond of work and that arguments are of no avail against their passions.[4]

Freud's conclusion was that, because of the social need for work, people will always have to be *coerced* into obedience to the rules of 'civilized regulations' (i.e. into social integration).

Like many other of Freud's general statements, this argument presents as a universal 'law of nature' a certain conjunction which has its beginning (and possibly also its end) in human history. The combination of work and coercion is indeed a 'social necessity', yet a necessity closely related to a specific type of social system, one characterized by coordinating human actions with systemic repro-duction through the institution of work. The 'decentring' of work inside the individual life-world may well render yesterday's necessi-ties irrelevant to the perpetuation of the system, and in a sense 'marginalize' coercion. The substitution of consumer freedom for work as the hub around which the life-world rotates may well change radically the heretofore antagonistic relation between the pleasure and reality principles. Indeed, the very opposition be-tween the two, depicted by Freud as implacable, may be all but neutralized.

Far from suppressing the human drive to pleasure, the capitalist system in its consumer phase deploys it for its own perpetuation. *Producers* moved by the pleasure principle spell disaster to a profit-guided economy. Equally if not more disastrous would be, however, *consumers* not moved by the same principle. Having won the struggle for control over production, and made its ascendancy in that sphere secure, capital can now give the pleasure principle free rein in the world of consumption. As a matter of fact, the conquest of production remains secure precisely because a safe (and bene-ficial) outlet has been found for the potentially troublesome drive to pleasure.

For the consumer, reality is not the enemy of pleasure. The tragic moment has been removed from the insatiable drive to enjoyment. Reality, as the consumer experiences it, *is* a pursuit of pleasure. Freedom is about the choice between greater and lesser satisfac-tion, and rationality is about choosing the first rather than the second. For the consumer system, a spending-happy consumer is a necessity; for the individual consumer, spending is a duty — perhaps the most important of duties. There is a pressure to spend: on the social level, the pressure of symbolic rivalry, of self-building through the acquisition of distinction and difference, of the search for social approval through life-style and symbolic membership; on the systemic level, the pressure of merchandising companies, big and small, who between them monopolize the definition of the good life, the needs whose satisfaction the good life requires and the ways of satisfying them. These pressures, however, are not experienced as an oppression. The surrender they demand promises nothing but joy; not just the joy of submiting to 'something greater than myself' — the quality which Emile Durkheim, somewhat prematurely, imputed to social conformity in his own, still largely pre-consumer, society (and postulated as a universal attribute of all conformity, in any type of society, ancient or modern) — but straightforward, sensual joy of tasty eating, pleasant smelling, soothing drinking, relaxing driving or the joy of being surrounded with smart, glistening, eye-caressing objects. With such duties, who needs rights?

Students and analysts of contemporary society have repeatedly expressed the view that thought and action of the modern individual are heavily influenced by exposure to the so-called 'mass media of communication'. They share this view with popular opinion; yet what they mean by the 'influence of mass media' differs sharply from the meaning implied by popular criticism of the media (TV in particular). The latter perceives the 'influence' in simple and direct terms: as making certain explicit statements which are believed the moment they are heard, or showing certain pictures of actions which are emulated when seen. Self-appointed guardians of public morals protest against scenes of violence or sex; they assume that the viewers' violent instincts and sexual appetites are boosted by exposure to such images, and encouraged to seek release. There are no conclusive research findings either corroborating or disqualifying such assumptions. What is, however, a most remarkable feature of popular fears related to the pernicious moral impact of television is that the possibility that the *total* presentation of reality through television, rather than separate programmes or scenes, is what matters — is not considered at all. One could observe that the inattention of the audience to this 'global' influence of mass media on their life-world is in itself a striking effect of the global influence.

It was the concern with the overall impact of television upon our image of the world, our ways of thinking about the world and acting in it, that was expressed by the Canadian media-analyst Marshall McLuhan in his famous phrase 'the medium is the message'. Encapsulated in the phrase is the rather complex idea that whatever the explicit message of the media is, the most powerful influence on the viewer is exerted by the way and the form in which the message is conveyed, rather than by its 'content' (i.e. that aspect of the message which can be verbalized as a series of assertions about the ostensible topic of the message). If what one knows about the world comes from the television more than from any other source, the world which is known will be in all probability a world consisting of pictures lasting for a brief moment only, of 'happenings', mutually unconnected and self-enclosed episodes, events caused and prevented by individuals pursuing easily recognizable and familiar motives, individuals helped by knowledgeable experts to find their true needs, the way to satisfy them and the model of happiness.

Martin Esslin set himsef the task of finding out exactly what sort of a 'message' the medium of television is. Here is his conclusion: 'whatever else it might present to its viewers, television as such displays the basic characteristics of the dramatic mode of communication — and *thought*, for drama is also a method of thinking, of experiencing the world and reasoning about it'.

Now the 'dramatic mode of communication' is distinguished by a number of traits, each of direct importance to the consumer way of life, to that unique alliance between traditionally hostile reality and pleasure, to that remarkable mode of being where freedom need not be paid for with pangs of insecurity. Let us name but a few, following Esslin's suggestions. To start with, 'Real events happen only once and are irreversible and unrepeatable: drama looks like a real event but can be repeated at will'. News is sandwiched between two pieces of dramatized stories, with which it shares the presentation of events as essentially repeatable; happenings which may be seen again and again, in fast or slow motion, from this angle or another; happenings which for this reason are always inconclusive, 'until further notice', never final and irrevocable; events which are much like a 'having-another-go' kind of experience (remember Judas asking Christ 'can we start again, please?' in *Jesus Christ, Superstar*? This is the kind of question which can be asked only in the television age). The world split into a multitude of mini-dramas has a distinctive mode of existence, but no clear-cut direction. This is a 'soft' world, where actions are just successive episodes among many others before and after, have consequences which are temporary and redeemable, and hence have no undue moral responsibility attached. Moreover, 'Drama is always action; its action is always that of human beings. In drama we experience the world through personality . . . what we hear is always spoken by a specific individual and has value only as his or her pronouncement'.[5] Events are what the individuals do. They happen because they have been chosen to happen. They could have been chosen differently, or not chosen at all. Their ultimate meaning, therefore, is the individual motive which caused them to happen. There is a free-choosing, motivated individual behind every event, and the world is but a series of events. The world is just a collection of options and choices — exactly like the life-world of the free consumer. The two worlds wink at each other, replicate each other, legitimate and confirm each other.

Some recent studies insist that television does more than *present* the 'real world' as drama; it *makes* it into a drama, it *shapes* it in the image of drama-like events. Under the impact of television, the 'real world' *becomes* indeed *like* a stage drama. Many 'real' events happen only because of their potential 'televisability': it is well known that public figures, politicians and terrorists alike, 'play for television', motivated by the hope that television will transform their private actions into public events, and aware of the difference to their impact this will make. What is somewhat less understood however, is that more and more events 'exist' only in and through television. In the opinion of Benjamin Barber, 'It is difficult to imagine the Kennedy generation, the '60s, Watergate, the Woodstock generation, or even the Moral Majority in the absence of national television'.[6] Daniel Dayan and Elihu Katz suggest that the provision of television's own, original events slowly takes precedence (with enthusiastic cooperation from actual and aspiring public personalities and their publicity agents) over mere 'reproduction of events', or offering the viewer access to an event which would take place anyway but in which the viewer would not otherwise be participating. Such media events 'are not descriptive of a state of affairs, but symbolically instrumental in bringing that state of affairs about'.[7]

The fact that a growing section of the 'world out there' which the viewer learns about through the television is a world created by the television itself, acquires particular importance in view of the understandable tendency of the communication media to self-reference. Armed with a medium of enormous power, the world of professional communicators and entertainers expands well beyond its once limited, stage-confined territory, appropriating estates previously managed by, say, professional politicians. In the world as made by TV, 'communication people' are heavily over-represented (as are media events in comparison with events without media origin or destination). Inconspicuously, and in all probability unintentionally, events in the media world and their heroes are assigned the same, if not greater, weight and importance as those

outside; most 'knowledge competitions', for example, put a pre-
mium on the recollection of top-ten charts and the ability to tell the
difference between two performers, rather than on skills in
interpreting events in 'real history'. Indeed, it is not clear any more
what 'real history' is and where its boundaries are drawn.

The media world has, as it were, an uncanny capacity for
self-enclosure. Given that it also shows a clear tendency for spilling
over (and conquering) previously foreign-administered territories, it
may well become the only reality against which the experience of the
free consumer can and ought to be tested. Providing the media world
and the consumer's experience are mutually resonant, and supply
each other with a sufficiently powerful 'reality test', the consumer
orientation which guides individual life may quite adequately serve,
on the social level, as the principal factor of social integration.

The media world is vast and colourful enough to fill the field of
vision of its viewers from end to end, and to hold their attention all
to itself. There is neither demand nor room left for anything else.
Among things left outside is a large part of politics: the part which
cannot be easily accommodated inside the only world the media are
capable of portraying; all the more abstract, principal matters of
policy choices or historical trends which pertain to the systemic
rather than the personal dimension of human life, and for this
reason do not easily let themselves be translated into images,
passion dramas, personal interest stories. The only form in which
politics is admitted to the world of the media is made to the measure
of that world. Politics appears in that world as a drama of
personalities, as the successes or failures of individual politicians, as
the clash of characters, motives, ambitions, as another (and not
particularly exciting) staging of the perpetual and never-changing
human comedy. Endearing or repelling features of character, bold
or cowardly responses to the challenge of the opponent, the
apparent veracity or slyness of the politician, matter more than the
merits or weaknesses of policies — for the simple reason that they
are much easier to convey (and to convey interestingly) in the
dramatic code of the television. Having drawn all the attention
upon themselves, such personal non-essentials of politics leave
many a seminal political issue out of sight. Paradoxically, the flood
of information made possible by the mass media renders most
fundamental conditions of social existence invisible.

Exposed to the largest part of its citizenry only through
public-relations experts and public-relations events, politics enjoys

considerable immunity from public control. Much like Bentham's supervisors, it 'sees without being seen'. While this is not necessarily a condition planned in advance and brought about by conspiratorial design, it is certainly gratifying to the politicians. Keeping the public at a distance, so that it can see only such things as are meant to be shown, gives the politicians extra freedom and allows them to pursue whatever they define as 'being in the interest of the state', however unlikely the public would be to agree if it knew. Not relying as yet on the spontaneous selectiveness of mass media of communication, governments use other means to ensure that the realm of their freedom stays uninvaded: issues unlikely to command enthusiastic consent are classified as 'state secrets' and actively prevented from coming into the public eye. Ironically, such zeal often has effects contrary to the intentions: even dull, technical issues suddenly become 'media titbits' once it has been revealed that they were dealt with by the power-holders in an underhand, not-fully-by-the-book, secretive fashion.

It would be, however, a grave mistake to account for the 'disappearing act' of politics as a contingent by-product of the media advance. The progressive elimination of politics from the horizon of individual life has been greatly helped by the media revolution, but not caused by it. It cannot be fully understood unless the changing role of the state in the consumer phase of capitalism is taken into account. Arguably the most important among the changes is the slow demise of the once all-important 'recommodifying' role of the state; the retreat of the state from direct intervention in capital–labour relations, from its concerns and responsibilities in the field of reproducing wealth as capital and human individuals as labour, in a system in which capital domination rested on engaging the rest of the society as actual or potential producers. In our present system, society is engaged by capital primarily as consumers. This engagement, however, does not require an active intervention of the state. The production of consensus and the solicitation of appropriate social conduct are taken care of by the consumer market. Consensual behaviour is often accompanied by the approval of the free market and individual freedom of choice — but an ideological consensus is not among its necessary conditions. The market-orientation of individuals pursuing the satisfaction of their ever-rising needs is all that is needed for social integration. Neither is coercion required; people had to be forced to work at some stage of capitalist history (remember Bentham's view of the factory as one of the varieties of prison-like confinement), but no compulsion and certainly no violence is needed to induce participation in the market game. With legitimation no longer prominent among the state's tasks, and coercion rarely applied to sustain conformity, the disappearance of politics from the horizon of daily life is neither contrived nor regretted. Most of the market players are shy and wary of such political forces (parties, policies) as promise to 'repoliticize' the now privatized world of individual consumption and interfere in what has become a private affair between the consumer and the market. Such external regulation as they need, the individuals would rather choose and buy themselves. They would prefer to be regimented by doctors, lawyers or teachers of their own choice.

A. O. Hirschman distinguished two ways in which citizens may exercise control over the powers which dominate them, and called them respectively 'exit' and 'voice'.[8] The distinction seems to be very useful when applied to the interaction between consumers and wholesale or retail suppliers of purchasable goods and services; indeed, the consumers set a limit to the suppliers' freedom either by refusing to buy their commodities (exit), or through involving themselves more actively in regulating the structure of supply, through consumer defence associations or watchdog committees (voice). In both cases one can expect the suppliers to be influenced; they would, in all probability, attempt to modify their offer in accordance with the customers' demand. It is a less convincing proposition, however, that exit and voice methods are options open to the citizens who wish to exert pressure on their governments. Governments which do not need to mobilize and regiment their citizens would not be particularly upset by a massive exit from politics; on the contrary, they seem to have developed an interest in political indifference and the passivity of their subjects. Today's governments are more concerned with absence of dissent than with presence of support. A passive citizen meets the bill perfectly, as he refrains from doing damage; his help is not called for anyway, at least under normal, peaceful conditions. Exit from politics means an indirect acceptance of the type of government which has little to gain, and a lot to lose, from the active involvement of its subjects in the process of political decision-making.

The consumer market as a whole may be seen as an institutionalized exit from politics; or as a highly rewarding attraction, meant to encourage prospective customers to leave in droves the drab, unprepossessing world of political, bureaucratic regulation. The latter world stays just round the corner to keep the migration going and the prizes waiting for the migrants ever more alluring. Movement into the market is accelerated by both 'push' and 'pull' forces. People are disenchanted with overcrowded classrooms, the shoddiness and unreliability of public transport, long queues and the perfunctory treatment meted out by the overworked and underfinanced national health service; and so they think with relish of visiting 'a doctor of their choice, at the time of their choice', or sending their children to 'the school of their choice, administered by the educational authority of their choice'. The less satisfying, the more oppressive the public, politically managed arena, the more enthusiastic the citizens feel about 'buying themselves out' of it. If only they could, they would leave publicly owned, politically administered services behind. The more of them do so, the less muscle or sheer nuisance power is left in those who cannot afford the 'exit'. Less pressure is exerted upon the government to improve the work of the public sector and to make its services more attractive. And so the deterioration continues, and with increasing speed. Still more energy is added to the exit stampede.

Modern political science developed a 'median voter theorem', which says, roughly, that 'only those programmes which can command majority voting support will be approved'.[9] According to this theorem, governments shun allocating resources to minority groups, even if it is only these minority groups who need them badly and cannot do without them. Such an allocation would be highly unpopular with all the rest, that is the majority, who would see it as a burden which they, as the taxpayers, must carry. If the needs of a minority become truly unbearable and cannot be further ignored, the allocation is sometimes made — but only in a form which wards off dissent from those who do not need it. For instance, instead of comfortably financing the education of truly poor children and adolescents, a smaller grant (clearly insufficient for some, but excessive for others) is offered to all, or at least to a number sufficiently large to reach the 'median voter'. This is very costly, and governments would prefer not to make the allocation at all, and to placate the 'median voter' by cutting taxes instead. Only a truly considerable 'nuisance power' of a neglected minority may out-weigh this preference.

But the massive exit of the better-off makes the 'voice' of the worse-off inaudible — their 'nuisance power' small enough to be safely neglected. A massive clamour of approval for such neglect would further stifle whatever voice of protest might be heard. With the 'exit' growing in volume and scope, and thus releasing governments from 'grassroot' pressure, those whose lives remain directly dependent on political decisions find that their capacity for 'making voice' (the practical chance of undertaking an effective political action) is fast disappearing. Meaningless in terms of democratic procedure guided by majority rule (as expressed in the 'median voter theorem'), their protest is matter-of-factly classified as an issue of law and order, and stamped out as such. The paradox of politics in the consumer era is that those who can make an impact on political decisions have little stimulus to do so, while those who depend on political decisions most have no resources to influence them.

There is a category of people inside the society of consumers who have slim chances of 'exit' from the obtrusive supervision of state bureaucracy and whose 'voice' cannot be made loud enough to be listened to. This category is made up of people living in poverty or near poverty through being chronically unemployed or employed only in casual, irregular and legally unprotected jobs, through being burdened with a large number of dependants, through having 'the wrong skin colour' or living in a 'wrong part of the country', that is a part abandoned by capital. In a society of consumers such people are socially defined as flawed consumers; their 'imperfection' (used to legitimate the discrimination against them) consists in their inability to enter the free-choice game, in their ostensible incapacity to exercise their individual freedom and conduct their life-business as a private matter between them and the market. Their 'imperfection', in typically circular reasoning, is taken as a proof that people of this category cannot make proper use of any freedom they possess, and that therefore they should be guided, monitored, corrected, or penalized for disobedience by those who know what is good for them and how they should have been using their freedom. Such a social definition is self-fulfilling. Once certain people do not know what their true needs are, their needs should be determined for them by others who do. Once certain people have demonstrated their inability to put their freedom to good use, their right to make decisions of their own ought to be taken away or suspended, and things should be decided for them by others. These 'others' are the state bureaucracy and the various experts it employs for the purpose.

In a consumer society, poverty means social and political incapacitation, first brought about by inability to play the role of the consumer, and then confirmed, legally corroborated and bureaucratically institutionalized as a condition of heteronomy and unfreedom. Poverty is related to income (too small by accepted standards) and to volume of possessions (too small to satisfy needs considered as basic or vital), which in principle can be measured in some 'objective' way (of course, the very idea that they can be so measured assumes that there are others — experts, men of specialised knowledge — who 'truly know' what is, and what is not, the condition of poverty). The state of poverty is not, however, defined directly by such measurable indices. In a consumer society, as in any other society, poverty is, in its essence, a *social* condition. Abel-Smith and Townsend suggested that the state of poverty is determined by the degree of 'social efficiency' (or, rather, inefficiency). A person in poverty is a person who cannot engage in social behaviour recognized as proper for a 'normal' member of society. Elaborating on this idea, David Donnison defined poverty as 'a standard of living so low that it excludes people from the community in which they live.'[10] Let us note that what does exclude people in poverty from the community, what renders them 'socially inefficient', is not only inadequate means of livelihood but also the fact that the state of heteronomy and intrusive bureaucratic regulation sets them apart from other members of the community, who are free and autonomous. In a society of free consumers, being told by the authorities how to spend one's money is a source of shame. 'Social inefficiency' is a matter of stigma — and being stigmatized makes one less efficient still. Sociologists who have studied the life of the contemporary poor all agree that a most salient aspect of living in poverty is the withdrawal of the poor from social interaction, the tendency to break old social bonds, to escape from public places into one's home, which now serves as a place to hide from the real or imagined threat of communal condemnation, ridicule or pity.

The bureaucratic determination of needs means a persistent lack of personal autonomy and individual freedom. Heteronomy of life is what constitutes deprivation in a consumer society. The life of the deprived is subject to bureaucratic regimentation, which isolates and incapacitates its victims, leaving them little chance to fight back, answer back, or even resist through non-cooperation. In the life of the deprived, politics is omnipresent and omnipotent; it penetrates deeply into the most private areas of one's existence, while at the same time remaining distant, alien and inaccessible. The bureaucrats 'see without being seen'; they speak and expect to be heard, but hear only what they think is worth hearing; they reserve the right to draw the line between the true need and a mere whim, between prudence and prodigality, reason and unreason, the 'normal' and the 'insane'. In the consumer society, bureaucratically administered oppression is the only alternative to the freedom of the consumer. And the consumer market is the only escape from bureaucratic oppression.

In capitalist society in its consumer phase, this escape route is open to, and taken by, a large majority of individuals, even if the residue for whom the escape is not accessible seems to be inevitable and permanent. There is, however, another — the communist — type of modern society, where the escape route in question is a viable proposition for but a small and uncharacteristic minority. In such a society, the bureaucratic determination and management of individual needs is the central principle, not a residual, marginal measure; so is the oppression, political incapacitation and forceful expropriation of 'voice' which come with it.

One way of conceiving of the communist societies (as they have emerged historically in a number of countries on all continents) is to visualize them as an extension of those life conditions which in a consumer society are associated with poverty, to the society as a whole. This does not necessarily mean that all members of a communist society live in poverty (we have seen that poverty is a matter of relative 'social inefficiency', and that the special character of poverty in contemporary capitalist societies derives from its being a 'deviation from the *norm*' — the norm being consumer freedom). This does not even refer to any particular, definite standard of living. It refers instead to the degree of influence the individual may exert (individually, as a consumer; or, collectively, as citizen) on his or her own needs and their satisfaction. The 'life conditions' in question, which are extended to the society as a whole, are conditions of heteronomy, of limiting the individual choice to the point of near-extinction. Most profound analyses of the communist-type societies seek 'the essence' of such societies precisely in the management of individual needs by the state. Ferenc Feher, Agnes Heller and Gyorgy Markus define the communist state as 'dictatorship over needs'.[11] What the needs of the individuals are, and how and to what extent they ought to be gratified, is decided by the political state, and acted upon by bureaucracy; the individuals whose needs are determined in such a way have little if any say in the matters of either the state or bureaucracy. They have, so to speak, neither 'exit' nor 'voice'.

The paltry, squalid life under communism, the notorious short-age of consumer goods, the enormous amount of time needed to obtain even the most elementary goods, are often explained as the result of the ineptitude of planners, the insufficiency of incentives to work well, or general corruption. The question is, however, whether the conspicuous absence of consumer freedom and of a proper setting for its development is a manifestation of a certain 'malfunctioning' of the poorly administered system or the essential principle of its administration. One can argue that the latter is the case: that the communist system represents an alternative to a society integrated through the consumer market and that the absence of consumer freedom is a most prominent and indispen-sable attribute of such an alternative. The political might of the state rests here on the state's ability to 'determine the determinants' of individual behaviour. This formidable ability depends on the absence of 'exit' and the suppression of 'voice'. A fully-fledged consumer market would provide an 'exit'; freedom to choose between conformity and dissent would make the 'voice' theoreti-cally (though not necessarily in practice) audible. Let us note that the ubiquity of political regulation penetrating the most inner recesses of individual life rebounds in the 'politicization' of issues which elsewhere would be of no interest to the state. Every personal problem becomes immediately a political issue; it cannot be solved without engaging some extensions of political power. An attempt by the individuals to use their own resourcefulness in coping with life tasks is potentially dangerous, as it undermines the principle of determining individual social standing by political behest; it is, therefore, perceived as corruption. If in the capitalist-consumer society the state can view the proliferation of political and social ideas with equanimity — as neither systemic nor social integration depend any longer on the universal acceptance of a specific legitimising formula — the communist state is shaken by every expression of intellectual dissent; offering no exit from politics, it cannot hope that the tendency to resistance-through-voice will dissipate by itself. The communist state must rely heavily not so much on the actual acceptance of its legitimizing formula, as on stamping out any attempt at political mobilisation of dissent; or rather, any manifestation of collective disaffection acquires immediately, from the state's point of view, the character of political dissent.

Our survey of the internal organization of the consumer-capitalist society, and its comparison with the communist society organized on a self-consciously opposite principle, suggests political-bureaucratic oppression as the only alternative to consumer freedom; at least, as the only 'really existing' alternative (as distinct from alternatives postulated as desirable but not subjected as yet to a conclusive test of practice or of theoretical plausibility). Moreover, our survey suggests that for most members of contemporary society individual freedom, if available, comes in the form of consumer freedom, with all its agreeable and not-so-palatable attributes. Once consumer freedom has taken care of individual concerns, of social integration and of systemic reproduction (and consumer freedom *does* take care of all three), the coercive pressure of political bureaucracy may be relieved, the past political explosiveness of ideas and cultural practices defused, and a plurality of opinions, life-styles, beliefs, moral values or aesthetic views may develop undisturbed. The paradox is, of course, that such freedom of expression in no way subjects the system, or its political organization, to control by those whose lives it still determines, though at a distance. Consumer and expressive freedoms are not interfered with politically as long as they remain politically ineffective.

The Future of Freedom. Some Conclusions

The competence of sociology ends where the future begins. The best a sociologist can do, when thinking of the future shape of society, is to extrapolate from its present shape. In so doing she or he is not very different from ordinary, reasonable men and women. Thinking of the landscape still hidden behind the horizon, we imagine it as similar to what we see around; we expect 'more of the same'. We do not know, of course, how well-founded our expectations are. Neither does the sociologist. Claiming otherwise, he puts his professional integrity at risk. Sociology has developed as retrospective widsom, not a modern version of soothsaying.

Inability to tell the future with the same confidence with which the story of the past is told, or present trends described, is not the fault of sociology. It cannot be blamed on the sociologists' disregard for the future or on a flawed methodology, fit to handle only such aspects of human life which have already sedimented or ossified as recorded facts. Quite independently from the moot question of whether an alternative methodology is at all conceivable, it would hardly make the anticipatory vision of the future significantly more certain. And this for a relatively simple reason: the human condition is not pre-empted by its past. Human history is not predetermined by its past stages. The fact that something has been the case, even for a very long time, is not a proof that it will continue to be so. Each moment of history is a junction of tracks leading towards a number of futures. Being at the crossroads is the way human society exists. What appears in retrospect an 'inevitable' development began in its time as stepping onto one road among the many stretching ahead.

The future differs from the past precisely in leaving ample room for human choice and action. Without choice there is no future —

even if the choice consists merely in refraining from choice and choosing to drift instead. Without action there is no future either — even if the action sticks to habitualized patterns and does not admit of the possibility of being different than it is. It is for this reason that the future is always not-yet, uncertain, open-ended.

It is only in this context of choice that sociology may be relevant to our thinking about the future. Sociology cannot tell us what the future will be like. It cannot even assure us about the outcome of our effort to mould it in a particular way. It cannot, in short, offer us *certainty* as to the future shape of our society — whether we wish to make this shape more to our liking or are just curious about 'how things will turn out in the end'. Sociology can, on the other hand, *inform* our choice (between this or that action, between action and non-action) by making us aware of the tendencies already evident in the present, of the shape of things they will bring about if left alone, and of the forces within society which make such tendencies work in their present direction. Sociology can also inform our choice by disclosing the consequences and connections of our habitual daily conduct which are all but invisible within the narrow perspective of our 'private', individual experience. In addition, sociology can inform our choice by making us aware that choice is possible: by pointing to alternatives to our customary way of life, which we may or may not find more hospitable to what we think our needs are. All this amounts to enabling us to make our choices consciously; to use, as well as we can, that chance of freedom which the future cannot but offer us. These services of sociology are for those among us who prefer to act consciously, even without the comfort of certainty of success.

We are now entering the realm of possibilities, not facts; not even probabilities of facts. Like all futures, the future of freedom is not predetermined. Among the factors which in the end will decide its shape, pride of place belongs to the direction human efforts will take. And this is something which those who make such efforts will decide.

Like all attempts to reveal an inner logic in the already-accomplished-reality, our analysis of the way our society works emphasized the 'systemness' of its mechanism, the accuracy with which individual way of life, social integration and stability of the whole 'fit each other'. Because of this emphasis, the overall picture did not augur well for the prospect of change. Consumption emerged from the analysis as the 'last frontier' of our society, its only dynamic, constantly changing part; indeed, the only aspect of the system which generates its own criteria of 'forward movement' and thus can be viewed as 'in progress'. It also appeared to play the role of an effective lightning-rod, easily absorbing excessive energy which could otherwise burn the more delicate connections of the system, and of an expedient safety-valve, dislocating the disaffections, tensions and conflicts continually produced by the political and the social subsystems into the sphere where they can be symbolically played out and defused. All in all, the system appeared to be in good health rather than in crisis. At any rate, it is capable of solving its problems and reproducing itself no less than other known systems could and systems in general are expected to. We have seen as well that the particular way of problem-solving, conflict-resolution and social-integration characteristic of our system tends to be further strengthened by the unattractiveness of what seems to be, from the systemic perspective, its only alternative. The system has successfully squeezed out all alternatives but one: repression verging on disenfranchisement emerged as the only 'realistic possibility' other than consumer freedom. Inside the system there is no choice left between consumer freedom and other kinds of freedom. The only choice not discredited by the system as 'utopian' or otherwise unrealistic is the choice between consumer freedom and unfreedom; consumer freedom and the 'dictatorship over needs', practised on the limited scale towards the residue of 'flawed consumers' or on a global scale by a society unwilling or unable to provide the allurements of the developed consumer market.

Half a century ago Aldous Huxley and George Orwell frightened the Western world with two highly contrasting visions of impending social transformation. Both painted pictures of self-contained and self-sustained worlds, worlds which knew of conflicts only as anomalies or eccentricities and swept the few remaining dissidents under the carpet. In all other respects Huxley's and Orwell's worlds differed considerably. Huxley conjured up his world out of the experience of the affluent pioneers of free consumption. Orwell, by contrast, took his inspiration from the plight of the first outcasts of the advancing consumer market. Huxley's vision is one of generalized content, pleasure-seeking and nonchalance; Orwell's, one of generalized (though stifled) resentment, fight for survival, and dread. The outcome, however, is again much the same: a society secure as to its own identity, immune to attack, capable of perpetuating its glory and its misery without end. In Huxley's world, people do not rebel because they do not want to; in Orwell's, they do not rebel because they cannot. Whatever the reason for obedience, both societies have guaranteed their perpetual stability through the most foolproof and expedient of measures: the elimination of alternatives to themselves.

Neither of the two visions fits the present system very accurately, though it would not take much effort to spot partial correspondences here or there. There is, however, a third vision, now 500 years old, laconic and sketchy by comparison with either Huxley's or Orwell's, yet reaching into the innermost essence of a system held together by consumer freedom. This vision we owe to a Franciscan priest, François Rabelais and his satirical masterpiece *Gargantua* the book which ends with the construction of the Abbey of Thélème. Thélème is the place of gracious living; wealth is here *the* moral virtue, happiness the main commandment, pleasure the purpose of life, taste the major skill, amusement the paramount art, enjoyment the only duty. But there is more to Thélème than sensual delights and the thrill of yet unknown titillations. The most remarkable feature of Thélème is its thick walls. Inside, one has no occasion to worry where the wealth, the happiness and amusements come from; that is the price of their constant and profuse availability. One does not see the 'other side'. Neither is one curious to see it: it is the *other* side, after all.

We can say that the consumer society took off where *Gargantua* ended. It has elevated the crude rules of the Rabelaisian abbey to sophisticated systemic principles. Society organized around consumer freedom can be thought of as an elaborated version of Thélème.

Thick walls are an indispensable part of consumer society; so is their inobtrusiveness for the insiders. If such walls appear in the vision of the consumers, they do so as a canvas for colourful, aesthetically pleasing graffiti. Everything truly ugly and unprepossessing is left behind: the sweatshops, the non-unionized and helpless labour, the misery of living on the dole, of having the wrong skin colour, the agony of being unneeded and wished out of existence. Consumers rarely catch a glimpse of the other side. The squalor of inner cities they pass in the comely and plushy interior of their cars. If they ever visit the 'Third World', it is for its safaris and massage parlours, not for its sweatshops.

Walls are not just physical. Perception magnifies the distance and deepens the separation between the sides. The insiders of the consumer society think of the outsiders sometimes with fear, sometimes with deprecation; with pity, at best. In a society organized around consumer freedom everybody is defined by his or her consumption. Insiders are wholesome persons because they exercise their market freedom. Outsiders are nothing else but flawed consumers. They may claim compassion, but they have nothing to boast about and no title to respect; after all, they failed where so many others succeeded, and they must still prove that cruel fate, rather than their corrupt character, bears responsibility for the failure. Outsiders are also a threat and a nuisance. They are seen as a constraint on the insiders' freedom; they weigh heavily on the insiders' choice, taxing the contents of the insiders' pockets. They are a public menace, as their clamourings for help forebode new restrictions on all those who can do without help.

On the other hand, the potential moral offensiveness of the walls is disguised by the moral indifference of the masks in which they appear in public. Walls seldom appear as walls; instead, they are thought of as commodity prices, profit margins, capital exports, taxation levels. One cannot desire poverty for others without feeling morally contemptible; but one can desire lower taxes. One cannot desire the prolongation of African famine without hating oneself; but one can rejoice in falling commodity prices. What all such innocuous and technical sounding things do to people is not immediately visible. Neither are the people to whom they do it.

Last but not least, why do the outsiders resent their plight? Because they have been denied the selfsame consumer freedom which the insiders enjoy. Given the chance, they would grasp it with both hands. Consumers are not enemies of the poor; they are patterns of the good life, examples one tries to emulate to the best of one's ability. What the poor are after is a better hand, not a different card game. The poor suffer because they are unfree. And they imagine the end to suffering as the acquisition of market freedom. Not only the outsiders' position but also the imaginable exits have been defined by the conditions inside the world of the consumers.

And so we return to the starting-point. The strength of the consumer-based social system, its remarkable capacity to command support or at least to incapacitate dissent, is solidly grounded in its success in denigrating, marginalizing or rendering invisible all alternatives to itself except blatant bureaucratic domination. It is this success which makes the consumer incarnation of freedom so powerful and effective — and so invulnerable. It is this success which makes all thinking of other forms of freedom look utopian and unrealistic. Indeed, as all the traditional demands for personal freedom and autonomy have been absorbed by the consumer market and translated into its own language of commodities, the pressure potential left in such demands tends to become another source of vitality for consumerism and its centrality in individual life.

Of course, the consumer-based system is not immune to challenges from outside. Societies where such a system has been more or less securely established constitute so far (and will, for the foreseeable future) a privileged minority in relation to the rest of the world. They have all transcended that threshold of commodity supply beyond which consumer attractions become effective factors of social integration and systemic management — but they attained this privilege through a disproportionately huge share of world resources and the subordination of the economies of less fortunate nations. It is far from clear whether consumerism may exist, on the world scale, as something other than a privilege. It can be argued that the privilege of today is the general pattern of tomorrow; it can be argued with equal force that the consumer solution to the systemic problems of some societies is more than contingently linked to the milking of other societies' resources. Whatever argument prevails, consumerism remains thus far a privilege, and as such is an object of envy and potential challenge. The mechanisms which make the consumer solution relatively safe from antagonistic forces inside the given society do not work on the world scale — or at least do not work in an equally effective way. Those who pay the price of consumer freedom, or those simply left behind in the race, neither can be dismissed as flawed consumers nor are they likely to define themselves as such. They may still think in terms of redistribution, one in which the game in which they feel systematically cheated may be itself a stake. It is to prevent such a turn of events that the rich nations are only too keen to assist the poor of the world in brutalizing each other. As long as they use the weapons generously supplied by the rich to maim each other in endless and senseless local prestige contests, the probability of challenge is kept below the danger level.

A challenge from outside apart, how likely is the consumer-based system to be reformed from the inside? As we have seen, the chance of such a reform does not seem great, in view of the self-perpetuating capacity of the system, which has found a virtual 'philosopher's stone' in the freedom of the consumer. With bureaucratic regulation firmly set as the only inner-systemic alternative to such freedom, the odds are that the kind of conduct which adds vigour to market mechanisms and thus reproduce its own attractiveness will persist unabated.

Before such a conclusion is drawn, let us recall, however, that the remarkable popularity of freedom in its consumer form derived originally from its role as a palliative or a substitute. Consumer freedom was originally a compensation for the loss of the freedom and autonomy of the producer. Having been evicted from production and communal self-rule, the individual drive to self-assertion found its outlet in the market game. One can suppose that at least in part the continuing popularity of the market game derives from its virtual monopoly as the vehicle of self-construction and individual autonomy. The less freedom exists in the other spheres of social life, the stronger is the popular pressure on the further extension of consumer freedom — whatever its costs.

This pressure may subside only if other fields of social life are open to the exercise of individual freedom; in particular, the areas of production, of community government, of national politics. Some sociologists point to the numerous social movements which regardless of their declared aims all demand greater participation of people in running their local affairs or in deciding vital issues of state policy. Some other sociologists focus on local initiatives, signs of growing interest in communal freedom from bureaucratic interference and a renewed drive to freedom not limited to individual consumption. Sociologists find such developments interesting and important, as they may crack the magic circle of bureaucracy and consumer freedom by introducing a third, heretofore neglected, alternative: that of individual autonomy pursued through communal cooperation and grounded in communal self-rule.

Freedom as the ability to govern oneself rather than 'being left alone' by the government, was the dream of those revolutionary movements which ushered the Western world into its modern history. The French Revolution of 1789 aimed at transforming that 'nothing' which was the 'Third Estate' (i.e. the great majority of the nation, denied effective influence over the running of national affairs) into 'everything' — into a force freely deciding all questions of public interest. The Founding Fathers of the American Revolution sought in their Declaration of Independence to 'guarantee a space where freedom can appear' — freedom again understood as fully-fledged and universal participation in public affairs. Commenting on the early experience of revolutionary America, Alexis de Tocqueville wrote of 'freedom for its own sake', justified by the sheer pleasure of being able to speak, to act, to breathe. The craving after a freedom which is not the right not to be bothered by public affairs but on the contrary an unconstrained and enthusiastically exercised right to manage them, is not therefore new. It has accompanied modern societies from their beginning. Yet it always remained a dream — a 'utopian horizon' at best. The real history of modern societies took a different turn. It led toward the 'exit' and away from the 'voice'. It brought the reduction of the public sphere to that where demands are addressed. It made personal autonomy and indifference to things public mutually dependent and conditional on each other.

A quarter of a century ago, in her profound study of revolution as a modern phenomenon, Hannah Arendt related the historical defeat of freedom in its public, active form to the unresolved problem of poverty:

> abundance and endless consumption are the ideals of the poor; they are the mirage in the desert of misery. In this sense, affluence and wretchedness are only two sides of the same coin; the bonds of necessity need not be of iron, they can be made of silk. Freedom and luxury have always been thought to be incompatible, and the modern estimate that tends to blame the insistence of the Founding Fathers on frugality and 'simplicity of manners' (Jefferson) upon a Puritan contempt for the delights of the world much rather testifies to an inability to understand freedom than to a freedom from prejudice. For that 'fatal passion for sudden riches' was never the vice of the sensuous but the dream of the poor. . . . The hidden wish of poor men is not 'To each according to his needs', but 'To each according to his desires'[1]

These 'poor men' of whom Hannah Arendt wrote are not necessarily people living 'objectively' in poverty, struggling for their biological survival, unsure of that minimum of nourishment and protection from cold which stands between life and death. Some of them are undoubtedly poor in this very sense. But there are many others who are 'poor', and bound to remain such, because what they possess is pitiful by comparison with what is on offer, and because all limits have been removed from their desires. They are 'poor' because the happiness they are pursuing is expressed in an ever-growing number of possessions, and therefore constantly escapes them, never to be reached. In this wider sense, not just the 'repressed' but also the 'seduced' are poor. In this wider sense, free consumers are 'poor' and hence uninterested in 'public freedom'. Instead of entrance to the public sphere, they seek its 'rolling back', they want it 'off their backs'.

Hannah Arendt blames the frustration of the revolutionary thrust toward public freedom on the unresolved problem of genuine poverty, which diverted politics to the 'social question', that is the provision of true freedom from necessity and thus the survival and subsistence of the people in need. This, in her view, brought the substitution of the ideal of individual happiness for the original one of public freedom. Gradually, freedom itself came to be identified with the right of the individual to pursue his own private happiness. In the general clamour for personal enjoyment, public concerns, the very wish of communal self-management, petered out.

What Arendt did not have time to notice was that the consumer society, born of the 'splitting up' of public welfare into a multitude of private consumer acts, developed the conditions for its own perpetuation. Whether it has or has not succeeded in lifting the 'genuinely poor' above the level of precarious and miserable existence, it has certainly transformed the overwhelming majority of the rest of the population into being 'subjectively poor'. If the link between (objective or subjective) poverty and the erosion of interest in public freedom is as real and powerful as Arendt suggests, then the chances of the progress of consumer society leading towards stronger pressure for the right 'to have a say' in running communal affairs look unpromising.

On the other hand, there is a widespread opinion among sociologists that 'communalism' (strong interest in what Arendt called 'public freedom') is almost a 'natural' tendency of the poor. It 'stands to reason' that precisely the people who are too weak, who do not have enough resources to secure their own living, to stand on their own feet, should be interested in making up for the dearth of individual strength through uniting their efforts and forces. In a recent highly innovative study of the dilemmas of living in an 'open', consumer society, Geoff Dench suggested that 'communalism', contrary to the individualistic 'humanism' of the well-off, is 'particularly relevant to humble folk — the "losers" in the open society. Communalism is a philosophy for the weak' (while the ostensibly universalistic, 'generally human' individualism of the élites is 'a philosophy for winners').

If there is indeed such a natural affinity between the plight of the poor and a tendency towards communal cooperation and self-

management, the rarity of the latter is a mystery. More puzzling still
is the absence of any clear correlation between the present growth
of 'objective poverty' and a growing demand for more 'public freedom'. Dench himself offers a key to this puzzle: he points out that
only those groups from which the strong members cannot readily
opt out are capable of supporting their weak.[2] Racially or ethnically
segregated populations are the most obvious examples of such
groups: for their individually successful members there is no 'way
out' from the group, however much they desire to get rid of the political, social or cultural deprivations associated with their ethnicity
or race. This is not, however, the case with other deprived groups.
The passage away from the group and into privileged status is not
barred. No artificial — legal or social — hurdles are erected, and
hence the road to a better life is privatized, much as everything else
in this kind of 'open society'. Individuals with the right amount of
industry, drive and cunning are invited to join the ranks of the privileged simply by 'buying themselves out' of the group burdened with
deprivations. Their departure leaves the group weaker and poorer
than before and less able to impress the urgency of its needs upon
the rest of the society. More importantly still, the group is left with
less confidence in the desirability of 'communalism', and of collecti-
vist strategies in general. Its experience shows convincingly how
much more effective personal enterprise is than collective effort.

Opinions on the prospects of 'public freedom' (freedom as full
enfranchisement of members of the community, as the right to
share in joint determination of the common fate) differ therefore.
In their analyses sociologists stress different factors and propose
different causal hypotheses. Yet the overall picture is one of
consumer, self-centred freedom remaining alive and well, coping
effectively with challenges, dominating the social scene and having
still enough self-propelling force to keep it going for a long time.

This, in itself, is not a clinching argument. Students of society
have been repeatedly warned by history against playing down the
future importance of phenomena on the ground of their current
rarity and relative weakness. It may well be that the human drive to
freedom will not be satisfied by market-led, private conquests; that
the energy now channelled into consumer rivalry will seek an outlet
in the more ambitious end of communal self-management. This is,
however, as yet an unexplored possibility. And the future being
what it is, it is not for sociologists to decide how realistic this
possibility will prove to be in the end.

Notes

Chapter 1

1 *The Works of Jeremy Bentham*, vol. 4, William Tait, Edinburgh, 1843.
2 ibid., p. 40.
3 ibid., p. 64.
4 ibid., p. 54.
5 ibid., pp. 44, 40.
6 ibid., p. 45.
7 ibid., p. 49.
8 ibid., p. 125.
9 ibid., p. 126.
10 Michael Ignatieff, *A just Measure of Pain. The Penitentiary in the Industrial Revolution 1750–1850*, Macmillan, London, 1978, p. 212.
11 *The Works*, p. 50.
12 Compare Michel Crozier, *The Bureaucratic Phenomenon*, University of Chicago Press, Chicago, 1964; also: W. Ross Ashby, 'The Application of Cybernetics as to Psychiatry', in Alfred G. Smith, (ed.), *Communication and Culture*, Harcourt, Brace, Jovanovich, New York, 1966.
13 Peter L. Berger, *The Capitalist Revolution: Fifty Propositions about Prosperity, Equality, and Liberty*, Gower, Aldershot 1987, p. 66.
14 I have discussed this process at length in *Legislators and Interpreters*, Polity Press, London, 1987.

Chapter 2

1 Louis Dumont, *Essays on Individualism: Modern Ideology in Anthropological Perspective*, University of California Press, Berkeley, 1986, pp. 106–7.
2 Peter L. Berger, *The Capitalist Revolution*, Gower, Aldershot, 1987, p. 19.
3 Colin Morris, *The Discovery of the Individual 1050–1200*, SPCK, London, 1972, pp. 2–4.

4 D. A. Wrigley, *People, Cities, and Wealth; The Transformation of Traditional Society*, Blackwell, Oxford, 1987, pp. 51-60.

5 Alan Macfarlane, *The Origins of English Individualism: The Family, Property and Social Transition*, Blackwell, Oxford, 1978, p. 165.

6 Edward Craig, *The Mind of God and the Works of Man*, Clarendon Press, Oxford, 1987.

7 Compare Robert Jay Lifton, 'Protean Man', *Partisan Review*, winter 1968, pp. 13–27.

8 Norbert Elias, *The Civilising Process: The History of Manners*, trans. Edmund Jephcott, Blackwell, 1978, pp. 256 and 260 respectively.

9 Niklas Luhmann, *Love as Passion: The Codification of Intimacy*, trans. Jeremy Gaines and Doris L. Jones, Polity Press, London, 1986, p. 15.

10 Joseph Bensman and Robert Lilienfeld, *Between Public and Private: The Lost Boundaries of the Self*, Free Press, New York, 1979, p. 62.

11 Andrew J. Weigert, *Sociology of Everyday Life*, Longman, London, 1981, pp. 115, 122.

12 Mike Emmison, *'The Economy': Its Emergence in Media Discourse*, in Howard Davis and Paul Walton (eds.), *Language, Image, Media*, Blackwell, Oxford, 1983, pp. 141ff.

13 Philippe Dandi, *Power in the Organisation: The Discourse of Power in Managerial Praxis*, Blackwell, Oxford, 1986, p. 1.

14 Jeffrey C. Alexander, 'The Dialectic of Individuation and Domination: Weber's Rationalisation Theory and Beyond', in Sam Whimster and Scott Lash (eds.), *Max Weber, Rationality and Modernity*, Allen & Unwin, London, 1987, p. 188.

15 In *Max Weber, Rationality and Modernity*, p. 11.

16 Martin Albrow, 'The Application of the Weberian Concept of Rationalisation to Contemporary Conditions, in ibid., p. 181.

17 Compare David Beetham, *Bureaucracy*, Open University Press, Milton Keynes.

Chapter 3

1 Barrington Moore Jr, *Privacy: Studies in Social and Cultural History*, M. E. Sharpe, Arnouk, 1984, p. 42–3.

2 John Lachs, *Responsibility and the Individual in Modern Society*, Harvester Press, Brighton, 1981, p. 58.

3 Orest Ranum, 'Les Refuges de l'intimité', in Phillipe Ariès and Georges Duby (eds.), *Histoire de la vie privée*, Seuil, Paris, 1986, vol. 3, pp. 211–14.

4 George Balandier, *Political Anthropology*, trans. by A. M. Shandon Smith, Random House, New York, 1970, p. 41.

5 Mary Douglas, *How Institutions Think*, Routledge & Kegan Paul, London, 1987, p. 25.

6 Bryan S. Turner, 'The Rationalisation of the Body: Reflections on

Modernity and Discipline', in Sam Whimster and Scott Lash (eds.), *Max Weber, Rationality and Modernity*, Allen & Unwin, London, 1987, p. 238.

7 Kevin Robins and Frank Webster, 'The Revolution of the Fixed Wheel' (Jeremy Seabrook): Information, Technology, and Social Taylorism', in Phillip Drummond and Richard Peterson (eds.), *Television in Transition*, BFI, London, 1985, p. 36.

8 Nicholas Abercrombie, Stephen Hill and Bryan S. Turner, *Sovereign Individuals of Capitalism*, Allen & Unwin, London, 1986, pp. 121, 151.

9 Norbert Elias, *Civilising Process: State Formation and Civilisation*, trans. Edmund Jephcott, Blackwell, Oxford, 1982, pp. 99, 106, 107.

10 John G. Canelti, *Apostles of the Self-Made Man*, University of Chicago Press, Chicago, 1965, p. 203, 207.

11 Quoted after Edmund Preteceille and Jean-Pierre Terrail, *Capitalism, Consumption and Needs*, Blackwell, Oxford, 1986, p. 21.

12 Compare Pierre Bourdieu, 'Distinction', *A Social Critique of the Judgment of Taste*. Harvard University Press, Cambridge, Mass., 1984.

13 Pierre Bourdieu, 'Conditions de classe et positions de classe', *European Journal of Sociology* 2 (1966) p. 214.

14 Compare Marc Guillaume, *Le Capital et son double*, PUF, Paris, 1975.

15 Martin Esslin, *The Age of Television*, W. H. Freeman, San Francisco, 1982, p. 85.

16 Michel Parenti, *Inventing Reality: The Politics of the Mass Media*, St Martins Press, New York, 1986, p. 65.

17 Douglas E. Ashfield, *The Emergence of the Welfare State*, Blackwell, Oxford, 1986, p. 13.

18 Quoted after Henry Hazzlitt, *The Conquest of Poverty*, UPA, Lanham, 1986, p. 81.

19 Brian Abel-Smith, *Freedom in the Welfare State*, Fabian Society, London, 1964, p. 3.

20 Jean Seaton, 'The Media and the Politics of Interpreting Unemployment', in Sheila Allen, Alan Watson, Kate Purcell and Stephen Ward (eds.), *The Experience of Unemployment*, Macmillan, London, 1986, p. 26.

Chapter 4

1 For a detailed analysis of the process, see Z. Bauman, *Memories of Class: Essays in Pre-history and After-life of Class*, Routledge & Kegan Paul, London, 1982.

2 Compare Frank Parkin's profound analysis of the 'closure through exclusion' tendency in *Marxism and Class Theory: A Bourgeois Critique*, Tavistock, London, 1979.

3 Claus Offe, *Disorganised Capitalism, Contemporary Transformations*

of Work and Politics, ed. John Keane, Polity Press, London, 1985, pp. 141–3.

4 Sigmund Freud, *The Future of an Illusion*, trans. W. D. Robson-Scott, Hogarth Press, London, 1973, pp. 3–4.

5 Martin Esslin, *The Age of Television*, W. H. Freeman, San Francisco, 1982, pp. 8, 20.

6 Quoted after Louis Banks, The Rise of Newsocracy, in Ray Eldon, Hiebert and Carol Reuss, (eds.), *Impacts of Mass Media Current Issues*, Longman, London, 1985, p. 31.

7 Daniel Dayan and Elihu Katz, 'Performing Media Events' in James Curran, Anthony Smith and Pauline Wingate (eds.), *Impacts and Influence Essays on Media Power in the Twentieth Century*, Methuen, London, 1987, pp. 175, 183.

8 Compare A. O. Hirschman, *Exit, Voice, and Loyalty*, Harvard University Press, Cambridge, Mass, 1970.

9 Patrick Donleavy and Brandon O'Leary, *Theories of the State: The Politics of Liberal Democracy*, Macmillan, London, 1987, p. 109.

10 Quoted after Stein Ringer, *The Possibility of Politics: A Study in the Political Economy of the Welfare State*, Clarendon Press, Oxford, 1987, p. 144.

11 Ferenc Feher, Agnes Heller and Gyorgy Markus, *Dictatorship over Needs*, Oxford University Press, Oxford, 1983.

Chapter 5

1 Hannah Arendt, *On Revolution*, Faber & Faber, New York, 1963, pp. 135–6.

2 Geoff Dench, *Minorities in the Open Society: Prisoners of Ambivalence*, Routledge & Kegan Paul, London, 1986, pp. 180, 184.

Suggestions for Further Reading

Meaning and function of freedom in its contemporary form cannot be truly understood without a knowledge of the sweeping economic, political and cultural transformations which are associated with the concept of 'modernity' and its present crisis. Surveys of these processes can be found in Peter L. Berger, *The Capitalist Revolution* (Gower, Aldershot, 1987); Norbert Elias, *The Civilising Process, State Formation and Civilisation* (Blackwell, Oxford, 1982); and Sam Whimster and Scott Lash (eds.), *Max Weber, Rationality and Modernity* (Allen & Unwin, London, 1987). Profound analyses of crucial processes which define the current stage of modernity are contained in Claus Offe, *Disorganised Capitalism, Contemporary Transformations of Work and Politics* (Polity Press, London, 1985); Frank Parkin, *Marxism and Class Theory* (Tavistock, London, 1979); and David Beetham *Bureaucracy* (Open University Press, Milton Keynes, 1987). Patrick Dunleavy and Brendan O'Leary, *Theories of the State, The Politics of Liberal Democracy* (Macmillan, London, 1987) is a lucid introduction to the theories of modern politics.

Seminal information on the sociogenesis of modern freedom may be gleaned from Louis Dumont, *Essays on Individualism* (University of Chicago Press, Chicago, 1986); Barrington Moore Jr, *Privacy, Studies in Social and Cultural History* (M. E. Sharpe, Arnouk, 1984) and Michael Ignatieff, *The Needs of Strangers* (Chatto & Windus, London, 1984). The peculiarities of the British history of freedom are subjected to a thorough scrutiny in Alan Macfarlane, *The Origins of English Individualism* (Blackwell, Oxford, 1978) and D. A. Wrigley, *People, Cities, and Wealth* (Blackwell, Oxford, 1987). Nicholas Abercrombie, Stephen Hill and Bryan S. Turner, *Sovereign Individuals of Capitalism* (Allen & Unwin, London, 1986) and Joseph Bensman and Robert Lilienfeld, *Between Public and Private: The Lost Boundaries of the Self* (Free Press, New York, 1979) offer an illuminating discussion of some basic antinomies of modern freedom.

Various aspects of the transformation of individual freedom in the rising consumer society are analysed in Zygmunt Bauman, *Legislators and Interpreters: On Intellectuals, Modernity and Postmodernity* (Polity Press,

London, 1987), John G. Cavelti, *Apostles of the Self-Made Man* (University of Chicago Press, Chicago, 1965); Elisabeth Loy, *The American Dream and the Popular Novel* (Routledge & Kegan Paul, London, 1985); David Madden (ed.), *American Dreams, American Nightmares* (Southern Illinois University Press, 1971). An interesting introduction into the complex issues of the theory and practice of modern consumerism is provided by Wolfgang Fritz Haug, *Critique of Commodity Aesthetics: Appearance, Sexuality and Advertising in Capitalist Society* (Polity Press, London, 1986); Rosalind H. Williams *Dream Worlds* (University of California Press, Berkeley, 1982); Elisabeth Wilson, *Adorned in Dreams: Fashion and Modernity* (Virago, London, 1985).

The first insight into, as well as profound interpretations of, the role played by modern media of communication in developing and sustaining the consumer form of freedom are offered in Andrew J. Weigert, *Sociology of Everyday Life* (Longman, London, 1981); Liisa Uumitalo (ed.), *Consumer Behaviour and Environmental Quality* (Gower, Aldershot, 1983); Martin Esslin, *The Age of Television* (W. H. Freeman, San Francisco, 1982); Ray Eldon Hiebert and Carol Reuss (eds.), *Impact of Mass Media* (Longman, London, 1985); and James Curran, Anthony Smith and Pauline Wingate (eds.), *Impacts and Influences: Essays on Media Power in the Twentieth Century* (Methuen, London, 1987).

The poverty and repression which constitute the other side of modern consumerism are explored in Claus Offe, *Contradictions of the Welfare State* (Hutchinson, London, 1984); Zygmunt Bauman, *Memories of Class* (Routledge & Kegan Paul, London, 1982); Sir John Walley *Social Security: Another British Failure?* (Charles Knight, 1972); Henry Hazzlitt, *The Conquest of Poverty* (UPA, Lanham, 1973), Stein Ringen *The Possibility of Politics* (Clarendon Press, Oxford, 1987). A shattering picture of the life of non-consumers in the world of consumer freedom can be found in Jeremy Seabrook, *Landscapes of Poverty* (Blackwell, Oxford, 1985).

Index